GUILT
ABOUT
THE
PAST

BERNHARD SCHLINK

GUILT ABOUT THE PAST

ANANSI

First published in 2009 by University of Queensland Press

This edition published in 2010 by
House of Anansi Press Inc.
110 Spadina Avenue, Suite 801
Toronto, ON, M5V 2K4
Tel. 416-363-4343
Fax 416-363-1017
www.anansi.ca

Distributed in Canada by
HarperCollins Canada Ltd.
1995 Markham Road
Scarborough, ON, M1B 5M8
Toll free tel. 1-800-387-0117

Distributed in the United States by
Publishers Group West
1700 Fourth Street
Berkeley, CA 94710
Toll free tel. 1-800-788-3123

Library and Archives Canada Cataloging in Publication

Schlink, Bernhard
Guilt about the past / Bernhard Schlink.

ISBN 978-0-88784-959-6

1. Guilt — Social aspects. 2. Guilt and culture — Germany.
I. Title.

BJ1471.5.S36 2010   170   C2009-906502-9

Library of Congress Control Number: 2009940186

Jacket design: Bill Douglas on The Farm
Text design and typesetting: Post Pre-Press Group, Brisbane

Canada Council   Conseil des Arts   ONTARIO ARTS COUNCIL
for the Arts   du Canada   CONSEIL DES ARTS DE L'ONTARIO

*We acknowledge for their financial support of our publishing program
the Canada Council for the Arts, the Ontario Arts Council, and the
Government of Canada through the Canada Book Fund.*

Printed and bound in Canada

Contents

Introduction

When we speak of guilt about the past, we are not thinking about individuals, or even organisations, but rather a guilt that infects the entire generation that lives through an era – and in a sense the era itself. Even after the era is past, it casts a long shadow over the present, infecting later generations with a sense of guilt, responsibility and self-questioning.

After the Third Reich, the burden of guilt about the past became a German experience and a topic of German cultural life and remains so today. Without relativising the national socialist past, it is true that the communist past is also a burden weighing on more than individual perpetrators and encompassing more than single acts. Even the student protests and terrorist attacks from the sixties to the eighties are sometimes regarded as the aberrations of an entire generation. That said, it is the experience and discussion of guilt about the Third Reich past that have infused the concept of collective guilt with its real meaning.

That the long shadow of past guilt is universal, and not just a German experience, goes without saying. But I'm not going to talk about the Americans and the Native Americans, the Belgians in the Congo, the British in India, or the French Foreign Legion. It's not up to me to judge other people's histories. Also, I'm just not able to discuss the shadow that past guilt casts upon the present in universal terms. Before attempting to think and talk about the universal experience of guilt, I would have to know much more about what other individuals have experienced and what their experiences meant in their native countries. I would never know enough – I have my hands full understanding the German experience.

The six essays presented here all have guilt about the past – Germans' guilt about their past – as their theme. The first one addresses collective guilt. How did it come to pass that guilt was assigned not only to those specific and singular perpetrators, inciters, and their accomplices who made themselves guilty by their criminal deeds – but to an entire generation? The second essay concerns the question of how one lives with a guilt-laden past and how such guilt can be overcome. The third piece builds on the second to discuss the role of law in this process. The fourth essay is about forgiveness and reconciliation – who can forgive and how can reconciliation be achieved? The fifth essay is a page from the history about the student movement of the seventies and how its effects reached into the nineties.

Finally, I would like to approach a discussion of literature more directly. In the first five essays I'll talk about it indirectly; I'll discuss guilt about the past and, even though it's a leitmotif in German literature and in my own fiction, I'll discuss it not as a literary leitmotif, but rather as a theme of political and moral discourse. This reflects my education and training: I am a law professor and was for many years a judge, never a literary scholar or critic. I might also confess at the outset that I don't reflect on my fiction writing in a theoretical way. I live with my plots and characters and play with them in my mind until I'm ready to write down the novel or story I have in my head. And since my characters think and feel within the parameters of my own thoughts and feelings, political, moral and philosophical themes enter into my fiction. But I haven't developed an epistemology of writing, and don't miss or feel the need to have one. In fact, the few reflections about literature and writing that I will try to offer in the last essay have only been triggered by the questions I have been asked and the criticism I have received long after the actual writing.

Collective Guilt?

Exploring the topic of collective guilt affords a view into the history of law. In ancient Germanic law, as in many other tribal law systems, when an injustice was committed it disturbed the peace between the individual perpetrator and the individual victim and, in addition, between the perpetrator's clan and the victim's clan. Thus, it was not just the perpetrator, but the perpetrator's whole clan that was exposed to the revenge or the penalty exacted by the victim and their entire clan. The victim's clan made the claim for atonement money, and the perpetrator's clan was accountable for paying it. This collective responsibility, liability, and atonement operated through all levels of society and affected adults as well as children. If the victim of the wrongful act was a child, then the revenge sacrifice chosen was often not the actual perpetrator, but a child from his or her clan. As a reprisal for a crime committed against the community, the perpetrator along with his or her partner and children might be deprived of any sustenance. Beyond this, children were legally liable for some of their parent's actions such as high treason and later also heresy. In the year 1320 in Nuremberg, a special law was recorded stating that persons constituting a danger to the public could be drowned in a sack together with their children. When families and clans were absent, and when the ties of families and clans became weaker, then the next highest-ranking collectives assumed responsibility, liability, and atonement; Germanic law recognised appropriate penal sanctions against guilds and municipalities.

Starting in the late Middle Ages the concept of collective responsibility, liability, and atonement lessened in significance. But even into the nineteenth century, when the notion had long since disappeared, there was discussion in Germany as to whether associations could be found guilty and were punishable for the acts of their members. And if I have informed myself correctly, Anglo-Saxon legal systems still recognise the imposition of fines against associations. Current international law prohibits collective punishments. It does allow, however, so-called reprisals to be taken against collectives that may contain elements characteristic of retaliation. A treatise of international law makes the subtle distinction that although the individual victim of the reprisal is being punished for a deed for which he or she is not guilty, this punishment is merely a reprisal vis-à-vis the collective. Of course, the victim will not feel the subtle distinction between a reprisal and a punishment.

There are a number of reasons for the diminished importance and eventual disappearance of the concept of collective responsibility, liability, and atonement. Today collective responsibility for an act is rarely included under the notion of guilt. Once guilt is defined as individual and subjective, based on fault, knowledge, and

intent, strict liability, based only on causation
and the result of the harm, becomes difficult to
understand and defend, even if it is the same
person who caused the result and is held strictly
liable. To find a collective guilty and to hold it
liable for something caused by a single person
becomes even more difficult to understand and
defend. The concept of individual and subjective guilt, or simply the guilt principle as the
foundation of liability, has become dominant
over a long development. In the first millennium, Christian theology developed a notion of
sin that focused on individual intent and individual reform. In the early second millennium,
Germany began to adopt Roman law in which
the individual provides the conceptual and
structural framework for judgment. Finally, the
individualism and subjectivism of the Enlightenment left no room for collective judgment.
Against this historical backdrop, the concept of
guilt in connection with collective responsibility, liability, and atonement can be recognised, if
at all, only as an irrational conceptualisation of
guilt. In a modern German legal treatise refer-
encing Carl Jung, collective guilt is understood

as a psychological phenomenon where guilt spreads itself from the perpetrators over the broader human and even physical landscape into the surrounding areas, seizing houses, villages, and woods where the crimes took place; it is as irrational as it is primal.

And yet, the development that gave rise to our current concept of individual guilt was fostered not only by the adoption of Christian theology, the reception of Roman law, and the growth and flowering of the Enlightenment rationality over superstition and irrationality. The disappearance of tribal liability or liability based on clan affiliation coincided with the dissolution of the tribe and clan system, which together with the decline of rural populations due to feudalisation allowed many to become, as was said in colloquial German, 'too low for the feud and too poor for the penance'. The increase of territorial rule and the monopolisation of the use of force by regional lords required that vengeful feuds had to be repressed. Whereas the individual had once been a legal entity not of his or her own accord, but only as he or she was recognised and protected by a tribe, clan, guild, or municipality, society transformed itself economically as well as politically, so that the individual now became the fundamental legal entity.

It was and is not irrational to have tribes, clans, and other communities that grant legal recognition and protection as entities that are thus capable of liability. The rationale for collective responsibility, liability, and atonement becomes apparent when we look at how old Germanic law approached the release from liability. The perpetrator's clan would be released from liability if they broke with the perpetrator, if they expelled him or her, or if they handed him or her over to the victim's clan. Not the least reason for this was that the perpetrator contributed to the clan's economic wellbeing. The clan was sustained by the labour and the performance of its members and ought not be able to continue to profit from the perpetrator's work. If abandoned to members of the victim's clan, this clan then had the discretion to either put the perpetrator to death or to make him or her their slave. In later times public authorities took over this role; instead of being delivered to the victim's clan, the perpetrator was handed over to the public authorities. Public authorities also punished the guilds and municipalities if they did not of their own accord punish, expel, or deliver a perpetrator up for punishment.

The idea behind these ways of achieving a waiver of liability is clear: the collective incurs liability for the perpetrator's misconduct in as far as solidarity and economic community with the perpetrator are maintained in reaping the profits from their labours, aiding them after the fact, and obstructing their just punishment. To punish a community because it did not administer justice itself by punishing the perpetrator or did not hand them over for punishment presupposes the existence of a public authority that hardly existed in early Germanic law and can be recognised in any real sense only during the course of the Middle Ages. But releasing the perpetrator's clan from liability through dissociation, expulsion, or ostracism of the perpetrator is an old idea, and the thought that collective liability has its foundation in freely chosen solidarity is discernable therein. This idea is something other than strict liability in opposition to liability through fault. It is not the idea of responsibility for someone else's crime, but of responsibility for one's own solidarity with the criminal.

The web of guilt that captures offences of this kind is high and wide. Beyond the perpetrators, every person who stands in solidarity with them and maintains solidarity after the fact becomes entangled. In a legal sense, today one can only be judged guilty if, according to existing law, maintaining or establishing solidarity amounts to criminal obstruction of justice, acting as an accessory after the fact, or receiving stolen goods. But the concept of guilt is not only associated with the standards of existing law, but also with norms of religion and morals, etiquette and custom as well as day-to-day communications and interactions. The unavailability of legal remedies does not exclude other norms from being identified and applied in other cases of maintaining solidarity with the perpetrator.

In my opinion, such norms exist. The maintenance and establishment of solidarity is a normative occurrence, supported and accompanied by normative expectations. By normative I mean expectations that are maintained despite factual disappointment and distinguished from factual expectations that are tested against reality and willingly modified when mistaken. Affirming one's solidarity with another is a declaration that they should be regarded, respected, and treated as an equal. In fact, as anyone can see, the two are in separate situations and therefore the declaration can be regarded as factually incorrect. Nevertheless, the expectation that both should be regarded as equals is not given up but held onto against the facts; one who declares oneself in solidarity with another is insisting on this expectation – as does an outsider who takes the declaration seriously. The price for establishing and maintaining solidarity is of course that one is regarded and treated equally also when one would rather not be. As long as the ties of solidarity are not severed, all the behaviour of the one will also be credited to the other.

The norms that bring about this connection of responsibility are not of a particular moral code or etiquette. They are the rules that communications and interactions follow and function under. If maintaining and establishing solidarity is not creating a community of responsibility, of answering for actions and ultimately of bearing the accusations and consequences then there is no such thing as solidarity. How is it achieved? By belonging to a family, an association, an organisation or institution, and even to a people. Not that the ties could never be severed, that there could be no dissociation and expulsion. Still, as long as those options have not taken place, the solidarity exists as by default, if you will.

The assumption that membership to a people engenders solidarity is something Germans of my generation do not easily like to accept. Many of us tend to regard ourselves as world citizens of a global society, as free citizens in a free world, as Westerners or Europeans, rather than as Germans. But everyone with minimal awareness who travels knows that the world is not so cosmopolitan and international as one might like it to be. That wish is symptomatic of another wish to escape feelings of common responsibility and guilt assumed to exist through the solidarity of belonging to the same country of people.

I would like to posit these last thoughts with regard to the Third Reich. The crimes committed before 1945 did not include only perpetrators, inciters, and accessories to the crimes; there were also those who were fully capable of resistance and opposition but did nothing. After the crimes had been committed it was possible to either maintain or withdraw solidarity from them. The perpetrators and those who were implicated in one way or another in the crimes could have either remained within the circle of solidarity or have been cast out if it. The legal historical perspective shows that the act of not renouncing, not judging and not repudiating carries its own guilt with it. And it is not a legal historical reminiscence. It is equally true today that one becomes entangled in another's guilt if one maintains or establishes solidarity with that person. The principle is as follows: to not renounce the other includes one in that person's guilt for past crimes, but so that a new sort of guilt is created. Those in the circle of solidarity who are themselves not guilty through actions of their own, bring about their own guilt when, in response to attendant accusations, they do not respond by dissociating themselves from those who are guilty. According to this principle it was possible for Germans, if not already guilty as perpetrators and participants prior to 1945, to be implicated in guilt thereafter for not having separated themselves from the perpetrators and participants though renunciation. That the Germans did not do so, or only did so haphazardly and half-heartedly and not as they were in a position to have done, is true without a doubt. They didn't even do it when they, as the German protestant churches did, recognised collective guilt after the war; whilst acknowledging everyone's guilt and seeking forgiveness for all, they neglected to renounce individual perpetrators and participants.

The webs of guilt have their own tragic nature, in the sense that dissociation, repudiation, and judgment could not be fully successful after 1945. For one, the numbers were huge; those who were involved in one way or another were just too many. And then there is the grim alternative between repudiation by 'a night of long knives' that would cut down both the guilty and innocent, and repudiation by the state governed by the rule of law through court rulings, case by case, that can only be insufficient in the face of organised crimes against humanity. There is no third choice. Even if the Germans had wanted to renounce the perpetrators and participants decisively and wholeheartedly, instead of haphazardly and half-heartedly, they would not have been spared the guilt: because renunciation would not have included all those who were guilty or because innocent people would have been implicated as well.

And the children? It is self-evident that the perpetrators, inciters, and accessories to the crimes are guilty. We understand also that those who did not offer any resistance or opposition in spite of being in a position to do so are guilty. We even understand that guilt also reaches those who do not actively separate themselves from the perpetrators and participants through dissociation, repudiation, or judgment. Finally, we understand that renunciation, if it had happened in a radical fashion, would still have produced guilt again and again. Still, is it necessary for children to find themselves entangled in this web of guilt as well?

After the considerations up to this point the answer appears obvious: if members of a community of solidarity bring guilt upon themselves by not renouncing those guilty members of their community, and if a nation of people is such a community of solidarity, then yes, children too become entwined in the guilt of non-renunciation. This guilt sits in wait for them until they become able to recognise the guilt of others, dissociate or not dissociate themselves from it, and therewith become capable of acquiring their own guilt. But I think that the conclusion is more complicated than that.

It has been observed that children whose parents experience guilt solely on the basis of not dissociating themselves after 1945, who were neither perpetrators nor involved in some other way, are usually free from feelings of guilt. The relationship with guilt that causes the norm of dissociating oneself does not appear to reach far enough. However, it is not the case that guilt has an effect only in horizontal relationships, i.e. among contemporaries, and not in vertical ones, i.e. between parents and children, since the children of perpetrators, inciters, and accessories to the crimes and, to a lesser extent, children of parents who, despite being able to, failed to offer any resistance or opposition, often experience feelings of guilt. Moreover, they experience the challenge of confronting their parents about their guilt and either coming to terms with it or withdrawing. Perhaps it could be said that the norm of self-dissociation extends to one further level of relationship only, horizontal or vertical, so that guilt emanates from perpetrators and other implicated parties to their contemporaries and to their own progeny, but not to the offspring of their contemporaries.

I would like to offer an explanation for this. The guilt of non-repudiation presumes a community of solidarity, which has to be actually experienced as a community inhabited by real people with whom one communicates and interacts. A community of solidarity is not something unintelligible or extrasensory, rather it is the tangible intertwining of relationships by real people as they communicate and interact. Seen in this light, belonging to a people in common is not wholly sufficient to establish a community of solidarity. It has to be concretely experienced, and it is experienced in an especially fundamental way: by belonging to one generation or one family, by living with one's parents and even grandparents. Living with one's teachers, pastors, professors and other respected and admired members of the parent generation can yield a similar experience of belonging. These experiences of belonging make the fact of belonging to a people in a community of solidarity personal. One's own identification with a people, its structures and history and the corresponding perceptions and expectations of others can likewise achieve this arrangement. But they do so only in decreased clarity and strength. What is more, one can avoid such identification and withdraw from it; one can live consciously in the here and now, not mired in history, and avoid contact with non-Germans, who confine one within one's German identity. The experience of belonging to one's own family or generation is inescapable, and for that reason the norm of dissociating oneself spreads at least as far as to one's contemporaries, to the next generation and even to the generation of grandchildren. But the dead grandparents who have been perpetrators are not family that is concretely experienced. To keep them within one's solidarity or to distance oneself from them is not an actual alternative for the grandchildren.

No judge can exempt, no verdict can free the children from their share of guilt formed as part of their parents' bequeathal to them. Maybe a psychotherapist or psychoanalyst could offer a sort of release. Obviously, repression can substitute for release aggravated by occasional feelings of dismay and self-consciousness, embarrassment and shame. In any event, over the generations, collectively experienced historical events become individually varied memories. The task of dissociation from specific historical guilt leads to the creation of one's own identity, an undertaking that every generation has to master.

Legal standards and the other norms considered in the course of my deliberations release the generations to come from guilt resulting from the crimes committed by the national socialists. To a great extent, they are released into the future with the freedom to decide for themselves whether to define their identity as arising from history or as defined only by the here and now. Insofar as they choose an identity saturated by history or one that other people assign to them, they stand in a certain sort of solidarity with past generations and will have come to terms with their guilty past, either by acceptance or dissociation. Only in this weak sense is guilt preserved in history and kept alive into the future.

The Presence of the Past

These years the people of my generation are turning sixty. We were born in the last years of the war and the first years thereafter and grew up with the German Federal Republic. We enjoyed the seemingly intact world of the fifties, grew tired of it and rebelled against it. In the sixties we became political, in the seventies we entered into our professional and working lives, in the eighties we grew successful in our careers, and in the nineties we secured influential positions in politics and government, the economy, education and the media. In a few years our star will begin its descent.

On our birthdays we give speeches about what we wanted to accomplish and what we achieved. Most of these speeches broach the subjects of the Third Reich and the Holocaust. For those of us employed in the humanities – in universities, culture and the media – the past, at one time or another, was or still is our topic; I don't know of any colleague of mine who hasn't, as I also have, given lectures and seminars on legal doctrine and practice in the Third Reich. For those of us working in politics, the administration, and the law, the past sharpened our understanding of freedom, equality, and a just system of government; the lessons to be learned from the Third Reich are an integral part of the advanced training programs for administrators and judges. When those of us in business or who offer professional services contemplate the ethics and responsibilities of their chosen fields they also contemplate the former involvement of these fields in the Third Reich and the Holocaust; they have organised exhibitions and publications on the role of doctors in the Third Reich, pharmacists in the Third Reich, chemists in the Third Reich and so forth.

For most of us our formative years were deeply influenced by the past of the Third Reich and the Holocaust. Its memory stood at the centre of our arguments with our parents and our rebellion against them. During the sixties, when those actually involved were reluctant to speak of the past, we developed a strong need to confront them, provoke them, ask them what they had done. Some of you may have seen the film, *The Nasty Girl*, in which a schoolgirl assigned to write a paper about her town decides to explore its wartime history, and encounters massive hostility from her older neighbours – this was a common experience among my friends. We regarded it as self-evident that the past had to be talked about, researched, taught, learned. Our image of German history acquired its contours from its shadow. When travelling abroad we were confronted as heirs of this past, and such confrontations came to define our experience of ourselves as Germans. Dealing with the past became a part of our self-perception and self-expression, even if it only played a minor role in our work.

Hence, for my generation the past is still very present – and not just for the intellectuals.

Two summers ago, during the soccer World Cup, I was watching a match in a beer garden in Berlin. When the German team scored its first goal, a worker my age threw his arms into the air and shouted, '*Wir sind wieder wer*!' ('We are somebody again!'). So even this worker saw himself under the long shadow of the past and experienced this moment as a liberation, as a chance to get back into the light. Since the expectations and ideas of our generation now define the cultural mainstream, the past that has moulded us and still occupies our thoughts has found its way into every corner of public life.

That was not without risk. During the sixties, the public discussion about the Third Reich and the Holocaust had to be insisted upon against great resistance. To break down the resistance of those who would rather have repressed and forgotten the past, the topic had to be raised again and again. But even after there was no longer anyone who needed to be convinced that the past may never be repressed or forgotten, my generation still prided itself on its moral fortitude. And it kept discussing the past as if doing so still demanded courage, still justified pride, still could not happen often enough.

The result has been a sort of banality. The Holocaust has become small change that is easily handed out. Yet another memorial event, conference, article or book against forgetting the past, another comparison between Auschwitz and some awful contemporary event. The analogies stretch far; I have seen Kosovo and Darfur compared to Auschwitz, Saddam Hussein to Hitler, East German border guards who patrolled the Berlin Wall to concentration camp murderers, and current prejudices against foreigners to those against Jews back then.

The legacy for the next generation is dangerous. The ennui sometimes exhibited by schoolchildren concerning the Third Reich and the Holocaust has its roots in the deadening frequency with which they are confronted with the past by their teachers and the media. Likewise, the careless to cynical tone they sometimes adopt in speaking about the past is partly a result of being steeped in comparisons whose heavy tone of moral pathos does not always carry a corresponding moral weightiness.

That is not to say that comparisons may never be drawn. The idea of the Holocaust as incomparably unique is as fatally belittling as inappropriate comparisons. In hindsight, the so called *Historikerstreit* (Historian's Fight) of the eighties, in which German historians and philosophers debated whether the Holocaust was unique, or could be compared to other events, looks almost absurd. Historical situations are always unique and can still be compared; comparing situations doesn't cancel their uniqueness. The historians and philosophers who insisted on the incomparable uniqueness of the Holocaust, because they feared that otherwise the Holocaust would lose its power as a warning signal to future generations, defeated their own purpose. Future generations can be warned by the Holocaust not to do something they are about to do only if what they are about to do is somehow comparable to the Holocaust. One can learn from history and from the Holocaust only if one compares.

If a situation is so unique that it can't be compared to anything, increasing historical distance will mean that it can no longer concern or engage us. It has lost its actuality. If the situation is discussed with moral pathos, that moral pathos amounts to almost nothing. Moral pathos not undergirded by moral engagement, and moral engagement not carried by contemporary concern, are not genuine. And the next generation keenly senses that hollowness.

What is both historically unique and persistently disturbing about the Holocaust is that Germany, with its cultural heritage and place among civilised nations, was capable of those kinds of atrocities. It elicits troubling questions: if the ice of a culturally-advanced civilisation upon which one fancied oneself safely standing was in fact so thin at that time, then how safe is the ice we live upon today? What protects us from falling through it? Individual morality? Societal and state institutions? Has the ice grown thicker with time or has the passage of time only allowed us to forget how thin it really is?

These questions concern the very foundations of our individual moral existence and our ability to live together in our society and its institutions. They are questions that are unsettling and challenging even after decades of relative safety within the political, economic and cultural realms of a civil society. At the same time, we are not confronted with, nor do we have to find answers for, these questions on a daily basis. Perhaps there are no answers for them other than living our lives with accountability for what we have been given: our relationships with other human beings, our work and our institutions.

This brings me to the next danger resulting from my generation's preoccupation with the Third Reich and the Holocaust. The lesson we drew from the past was a moral one rather than an institutional one. We accused our parents, teachers, professors and politicians of blindness, cowardice, opportunism, the ambitious and ruthless pursuit of their careers, and a lack of moral courage. The accusations levelled placed the blame on individual moral failings, and within those indictments lay an implicit duty to embrace a higher standard of moral behaviour.

Therefore, those among my generation who became teachers attempted to instruct their students how to show civil and moral courage.

Some of you may have seen the film *Rosenstrasse* about the wives who demonstrated against the deportation of their Jewish husbands until the deportation was cancelled. It is a movie that teachers love to see with their students. It illustrates what they took to be the lesson from the past: it is righteous to show moral courage and resist. It is righteous to fight the beginnings of evil because courage has a better chance then than later. It is righteous to prepare oneself for possible future situations by looking at past situations and pondering what one would have done in them.

Certainly, moral courage is one of the lessons gleaned from the past. But I have doubts about the extent to which it can be taught in this didactic way. I think it is learned mostly from living example, experience and repeated practice. Fighting and winning yesterday's moral battles with bravery in one's mind doesn't necessarily prepare one for today's moral conflicts. After the wall had come down and the question came up which East German judges could be accepted as judges in the unified Germany, the president of the Federal Administrative Court advocated a generous acceptance policy. He received a petition from West German judges who objected to this generosity: since East German judges had not shown the courage of insisting on their judicial independence but rather followed party orders, they were unsuited to be independent judges under the rule of law. So far so good. But since the West German judges didn't want to upset the president whose opinion was important for their careers, they decided not to sign the petition with their names but rather turn it in as an anonymous collective petition. They had learned something and they had done something but obviously they had also missed something.

Even if learned properly, moral courage is not the only and maybe not even the first lesson to be gleaned from the past. What the past likewise so glaringly shows is the helplessness of individual morality in the absence of institutions in which citizens are recognised and matter, institutions that they can impact by their appeals and which they can depend on to respond and support. Once parties, unions and associations, churches and clubs, universities, schools and courts have been forced into line, there comes a point when the ethics of opposition survive only in quixotic heroic gestures.

In as far as there was any resistance during the Third Reich and the Holocaust that had an effect beyond being symbolic gestures, its basis was found less in individual morality than in communist or socialist solidarity, Christian faith and ecclesiastic responsibility, and the honour code of officers or of the aristocracy. The lessons of the past pertain not just to individual morality, but also, and perhaps more importantly, to societal and state institutions in which individual morality must be preserved if it is to have the power to resist in the crucial moment. This applies to citizens' engagement within and on behalf of institutions to ensure their proper functioning. That does not mean, however, that well-functioning institutions are built on constant evocations of morality. Moralising appeals in politics, moralising arguments in court decisions, moralising sermons in churches on all aspects of life, and moralising lectures about the responsibilities of schools and universities are again wrong-minded remnants of the past. Properly functioning institutions embody morality without constantly preaching it.

Again, the engagement within and on behalf of institutions is something not taught and learned easily. Among my students I have many who strive for excellence because they want to go into corporate law and become rich. I have students who care about justice and human rights and want to work for non-government organisations, the United Nations (UN) and affiliated international organisations. I have students who want to enjoy the quietness and reliability of life as a civil servant or a judge, because today this life allows best for combining professional life and family life. But a judgeship at home needs and deserves as much engagement with justice as a job with the UN in Africa, and being an excellent lawyer in government, the administration, a union, or the church may not make you as rich, but is certainly as much fun as excelling in a corporate law firm. And the lesson from the past is that the maintenance of these and other institutions is as crucial a vaccine as assertions of individual morality.

Is this what it means to come to terms with the past, *die Vergangenheit zu bewältigen*? Contemplating what the past teaches us about life on thin ice?

The longer we live with the idea that the past is something we can and must come to terms with, the more paradoxical this proves to be. *Bewältigen*, which is probably translated most closely as 'to master' in the original and correct sense of the word, applies to a task; it stands before us, we set to work on it, and finally it is finished and mastered. Then we are done with it.

The thought that the past could and should be mastered contains not only the yearning for freedom from it; it even asserts an entitlement to such an end. As with every task, whoever works hard at it expects that the task will eventually be completed, and then demands to be released from duty once the task is finished. Whoever vigorously applies him- or herself to the work of commemorative remembrance wishes to be held captive by the past no more. Whoever remembers wants the right to forget.

The paradox becomes palpable when members of my generation, who are especially sensitive to issues of the past and are actively engaged in its commemoration, leave their home country. Somewhere abroad they run into reprobation on account of the past and they are incensed: they have delved into the problems of the past with such sensitivity and commitment – how dare those outsiders hold them accountable for it?

And yet, longing not to be chained to a traumatic past is not wrong. What is mistaken, however, is the idea that fixation on the traumatic past would somehow guarantee being set free from it. A collective past, like that of an individual, is traumatic when it is not allowed to be remembered, and is just as much so if it has to be remembered. In other words, fixation on the past is merely the flipside of repression. Detraumatisation is the process of becoming able to both remember and forget; it is leaving the past in the past, in a way that embraces remembrance as well as forgetting. This applies in the same way to the victims and their descendants as to the perpetrators and their descendants. Detraumatisation can only fully succeed if it is successful on both sides, but for it to happen and be successful across the divide can only be hoped for, with no expectations harboured.

There is no entitlement to having the victims and their descendants lay aside the past once the Germans have shown exemplary efforts in coming to terms with it. How and what they remember and forget, to what lengths they go in attempting to free themselves from the traumatic past through mourning the victims or accusing the perpetrators or claiming restitution from the perpetrators' descendants is their business. Whatever course of action they follow – it is not for us Germans to raise objections or feel indignation. Instead we owe respect to the other side's difficult struggle with a past that we made traumatic for them.

We must accept what they do but we do not always have to comply with it. An accusation made on behalf of the victims is not true solely because it was made on their behalf, restitution must not be paid simply because restitution has been claimed. Still, though the law may not require it, there are cases where respect and tact may require restitution to be paid even when it is not due, in consideration for their sensitivity, as well as for the perception of the world. It makes sense even though it goes beyond what is required in a strictly legal sense. It pays tribute to the fact that the past is still traumatic to others. It does not mean that it has to be traumatic for us to the same extent. Detraumatisation takes place concomitantly within the dialogue and on each side independently, and one side does not have to wait until the other side successfully completes the process. Waiting for each other can also keep both mutually mired in trauma.

There is no mastering the past. But there is living consciously with present-day questions and emotions that the past releases. Questions and emotions – of course the past does not just trigger questions, but also makes us lose our composure, be at a loss for words, and become sad, fearful, and enraged, despair of cosmic and human justice, and suffer under the guilt that ensnares not only those who were then perpetrators, but those who later tolerated the perpetrators living among them.

In the instances in which the past does not currently evoke questions or emotions nothing is gained by referring to it again and again.

38

This only devalues and squanders the past's moral legacy. Where the Third Reich and the Holocaust do not bring up the questions and emotions that our generation has experienced, the next generation will have to experience its own questions and emotions and in its own way. In any case, they will not have to confront some of the issues that the first generation and my generation faced; the third generation is only slightly caught up in the guilt of the past, and the following generation will not be at all.

Under no circumstances does the past allow itself to be dismissed. Not only because its horrors were so terrible that they can never be forgotten. Not only because it makes us perceive the threats to our cultural and civilised existence. It touches on all themes and problems of morality. Responsibility and conviction, resistance and accommodation, loyalty and betrayal, hesitation and taking action, power, greed, justice and conscience – there is not a single drama that cannot be exemplified by an occurrence out of this particular past with ample proximity to our present world and with adequate aesthetic quality.

Unlike Stalin's gulag and Pol Pot's killing fields, the Holocaust and the Third Reich are perversions of bourgeois culture and offer, moreover, this culture's universal content and structure in a perverted form. So the flood of books, films, plays, and performances dedicated to the Holocaust and the Third Reich will not cease for a long time to come, not in Germany and not throughout the rest of the world. And the past they encompass is global: the Holocaust and Second World War were the last historical occurrences that seized all the world at once, Germans and Jews, Eastern and Western Europe, America and even Asia and Africa. That past is our common history.

And so, the past is not lost, even without special efforts and events, even without the endless reproduction of what my generation started in the sixties and seventies, even without the next generation being confronted with the past to the dangerous point of becoming bored and cynical. Precisely because the Third Reich and Holocaust have become a universal experience and teach universal lessons they will not fade into obscurity. The past can become history for the generations to follow without losing any of its importance and impact.

When a collective occurrence, just as an individual one, is deemed as history, it no longer dominates the collective or individual narrative, but is integrated into it. With regard to the Third Reich and the Holocaust that means that German history does not have to be viewed as if everything in the past were building up to this particular outcome and would be fulfilled by it. It means that German history should not be evaluated in the present day only in light of those years, and that it should not be viewed and dealt with only from this perspective. It means that the literature of persecution and exile, so prominent in German literary scholarship since the eighties, can easily give up some of its prominence. It also means that the well-intentioned way in which German institutions take care of the Jewish legacy beyond what the Jewish community in Germany can afford and administer themselves should be more careful not to become patronising.

If something is wrong with one's biography, then one's sense of self and also one's relationships with others will suffer. What makes sense about the younger generation's often-heard wish to be able to be proud to be German is not that being German is in fact a merit one deserves to be proud of. One deserves to be proud only of what one achieves, not of what one is. But the younger generation's wish makes sense as an expression of the desire for a biography that allows for an undamaged sense of self and undamaged relationships with others. For these young people the Third Reich and the Holocaust can no longer be present the way it is for my generation, and if we would like them not to be dismissive of the past then they must be allowed to see the past merged into history. Instead of assuring the younger generation that they have the right to be proud or denying them the right, we owe it to them to integrate the past into our collective biography. The future of the presence of the past is history.

Mastering the Past through Law?

What is past cannot be mastered. It can be remembered, forgotten or repressed. It can be avenged, punished, atoned for and regretted. It can be repeated, consciously or unconsciously. Its consequences can be managed either to encourage or discourage their impact on the present or the future. But what is done is done. The past is unassailable and irrevocable. The word 'mastering' in its true sense applies to a task at hand that must be worked on and worked through, until it is completed. Then the task no longer exists as such. That the term *Vergangenheitsbewältigung*, i.e. mastering the past, is used and recognised in Germany but has no corresponding word in English and French reveals a longing for the impossible: to bring the past into such a state of order that its remembrance no longer burdens the present.

Roman law recognises the principle '*in praeteritum non vivitur*'. As a practical point of law it means that alimony cannot be claimed for the past but only for the present and the future. Its philosophical legal meaning is that we live in the present and into the future, not in or into the past; hence, the law governs and sets into order only present and future, not past, life. Of course, a judge can issue a verdict that awards compensatory damages or imposes jail time for an offence committed. Still, the compensatory damages are only an ersatz for the goods that were damaged or lost and the jail time does not make the offence 'un-happen'. Even laws with so-called retroactive effect do not actually work retroactively; they operate instead in the present and the future with a mere reference to the past. Since laws often refer to and have to refer to the past, the question of whether a law is truly retroactive is often difficult.

The notion that the past could be brought into form and order is foreign to the law. Law rests on the idea that at one point past acts are concluded and their consequences should therefore be settled. After a while the citizen has to come to terms with government actions or those of other citizens that he or she didn't fight legally or didn't fight successfully. After enough time, administrative decisions attain administrative finality and court decisions gain the force of law and can no longer be appealed. After sufficient time has passed, the statute of limitations prohibits state prosecution for most offences, as well as citizens' claims for damages. In a country under the rule of law, state prosecution of criminal offences proves unavailing when it pursues actions that were not punishable at the time they were committed. The difficult constitutional law question concerning retroactive application of the law starts with '*nulla poena sine lege*', a well-established principle that prohibits the legislature declaring an action a crime in hindsight.

Nevertheless, the law can be used to deal with the past in whatever way a society chooses. It can foster remembrance, neglect and repression. Criminal prosecution, restitution, fact-finding commissions and tribunals, and the granting of access to files and archives all support remembrance, while the granting of amnesty and the banning of certain topics and themes from public discourse encourage forgetting and repression. The law can rehabilitate citizens convicted of crimes, compensate for punishments suffered, repair destroyed careers and correct past decisions retroactively and it can likewise allow past sentences, punishments, decisions and careers to stand as they are. In every one of these instances the law is and was made to fit a given situation because some societies favour remembering, while others would rather forget.

In this rather narrow sense there is also a sort of mastering the past. The past is not simply the events that have happened but a construction of them in a manner that successfully integrates them into an individual or collective memory. The past is a construct, and creating that construct is a task to be undertaken and completed, at least provisionally, because new findings constantly arise from past events or new needs for integration develop. In this narrow sense the past is a task that will be undertaken regardless of whether it is reconstructed in a culture of remembrance, with partial forgetting, or in a culture of forgetting, with partial remembering. Moreover, the task must be completed. Individual and collective biographies require integration of the past as a requisite for the integrity of self-perception and identity. Past events must be integrated so that they are not played out against the present, thereby possibly damaging the current state of self-perception and identity.

There are many instances in which mastery of the past flows just as well through forgetting as through remembrance. Cultures of forgetting have appeared from ancient to modern times, and, for countries such as Spain with its Civil War, Russia with its Stalinist past, or Austria with its national socialist crimes, it is difficult to argue that forgetting and repression do not work. These countries have integrated the atrocities committed during a generation or more into their respective collective biographies and have achieved a peaceful transition to the next generation.

The law's instrumentality for overcoming the past through recollection as well as through repression, for fostering a culture of remembrance or a culture of forgetting, does not negate the fact that certain factors invite forgetting and make remembering difficult, while others invite remembering and make forgetting difficult.

The more recently an event took place, the easier it is to recollect and the more difficult to forget, the stronger the demand for legal redress and the resistance to legal amnesty. But once a first wave of remembrance and legal redress has occurred, a condition of exhaustion can set in, hindering the next wave. In Germany in the fifties, the first wave of remembrance and legal redress tapered off, partly because the Germans were exhausted from war, destruction, and expulsion, were weary of dealing with the past, and were concentrating the energies they had on new beginnings and reconstruction. That first wave would have tapered off even earlier had the Allied Forces not triggered and supported it. Again, after the fall of the Berlin

Wall the citizens of the new states in the East were exhausted from change and soon did not want to hear another word about privation and injustice in the German Democratic Republic (GDR). Here again, the legal proceedings that did occur regarding the privations and injustices of the former GDR were due to the outside impetus of the old West Germany. In any case, the Germans are not a people who revel in legal redress to settle accounts. The First and Second World Wars and the economic and political collapse of the GDR were experienced more as 'the slings and arrows of outrageous fortune' to be commonly borne, rather than as something that a minority of the Germans did to the majority and for which they now had to pay a price.

How recent or remote an event is is not its only measure of relevance. An event can be recent and yet feel very distant because then it was war and now there is peace; because it happened in a place far away and now one is home again; or because it happened under an old regime or during a revolution and now one is living under the new system. Two experiential worlds can, within short periods of time, be so strikingly different that it becomes arduous to map the past using the coordinates of the present. Because the world is constituted more along the lines of the collective rather than the individual, a collective need to forget will tend to overcome an individual desire to remember, and a collective need to remember will overcome an individual wish to forget.

Furthermore, if there is an 'other' who remembers and insists on remembrance, redress, restitution, criminal proceedings and verdicts, then that can become decisive for whether remembrance is pursued and done on account of the law. One individual has a difficult time forgetting if there is another who steadfastly connects him or her to an occurrence, a conduct or a crime. This is also true for a community that others identify as connected with specific happenings, conduct, and crimes; it cannot free itself by simply forgetting and repressing. Think of Germany, or more recently Serbia, Rwanda, and Cambodia on the one hand, and on the other of Russia and Spain – in the latter cases, forgetting and repressing work because there is no 'other', just Russians who had inflicted harm on other Russians under Stalin and Spaniards who fought other Spaniards in the civil war. The more numerous and strong those insisting on remembrance are, the less feasible forgetting becomes. Should they also be victims and should they be sufficiently numerous and influential then they can imprint their mark on the culture of the community and define it as a victim culture. Conversely, a victor culture could disregard a few, weak victims.

It is also, of course, harder for a community to be freed from identification with past injustices and crimes when a sufficient number of its members are implicated. Entanglement in the past arises not only through having been a perpetrator, an accessory, inciter or supporter. Common knowledge, observing and turning away, the omission of lending aid to the victims, not expelling, prosecuting, and punishing the perpetrators afterward, but seeing them instead tolerated or even respected – these all contribute. Solidarity with the perpetrator leads to entanglement in his or her crime and guilt – we discussed this as the centre of the idea of collective guilt.

Even given these considerations, the question still remains: does law, an instrument that can facilitate both remembering and forgetting, have an intrinsic proximity to either agenda? I will cite three often-used arguments for remembering as opposed to forgetting or repressing, be it in regards to the national socialist, communist, or any other horror-filled, criminal, and guilt-laden past. Then I will try to evaluate these arguments as to their claims on the law. According to the first argument, remembering is the secret of redemption. A second argument posits remembering and the work on guilt and grief as prerequisites for a strong individual identity, trust and solidarity in families and in society. The third argument holds that remembering is necessary in order to prevent us from repeating the past.

The first argument is the darkest. Remembering as the secret of redemption is a wisdom contained in the Jewish tradition, and rightly so within that tradition; without the will to remember the Jewish people would have lost their identity in captivity, diaspora and exile. But wherein lies the wisdom for those who didn't have to save their identity while being dispersed into the world? What does the wisdom teach beyond a collective's need to keep its collective memory alive?

Because of these questions, the wisdom is modified in the debates surrounding other past histories. The state of redemption is interpreted as opposite to a state of apathy. Apathy is regarded as dangerous because it is the opposite of hope, belief, and love. It makes people numb to what happens in the world, and especially to the injustice that goes on in it. Finally it allows people to lapse into complicity. Active remembrance could disrupt apathy, it could raise consciousness for the roots as well as the consequences of injustice; in a state of redemption humanity would not allow injustice to occur. Remembering becomes a prerequisite for not allowing what has happened, or something similar, to repeat itself – thus the first argument melds into the third, which I'll come to in a minute.

There are various considerations contained within the second argument, which states that remembering is necessary for successful familial, social and political relations. Psychologically, forgetting and repressing a traumatic past can serve to further aggravate its effects. Parents who keep their traumatic experiences a secret – be they perpetrators, guilty bystanders or victims – cannot express their individuality and offer their children openness and trust. Without learning openness and trust, their children cannot develop a resilient individuality that knows when to be steadfast and when to compromise. Second, there is the presumption that a generation that does not acquire openness, trust, and individuality in the family will founder in its attempts to achieve such qualities in society. These are not just relational qualities but skills upon which democracy depends. A democracy replacing a dictatorship would endanger its credibility, particularly among the victims of the dictatorship, if it did not punish the perpetrators and legally prevent them from retaining their positions and further pursuing their careers. Here the goal of punishment and other legal sanctions would serve to strengthen civic virtues and, again, prevent the past from repeating itself.

The third argument directly addresses the goal of preventing the past from repeating itself. It takes punishment as a deterrent that aims to prevent criminal events from being repeated by influencing individual perpetrators or even the society as a whole – if all of its members had been involved in the crimes of the past then all have to be deterred from committing them again. But applied in cases of atrocious political systems the theory of preventive punishment is rather weak. The conformist who committed crimes that were within the legal bounds of a past political system will still be a conformist under the new system and does not need to be deterred from what does not conform to the new system. Also, he or she does not need to be re-socialised; in the former political system the conformist comported themselves in accordance with the strictures of society and will do so again in the new society. When national socialist crimes were being prosecuted and sentenced, the perpetrators were regularly found to be leading normal lives after 1945 and could exhibit great neighbourly, collegial friendliness, reliability, and good will. Thus, in a society where an old political system has failed and a new political system has taken hold its people do not really need to be deterred from acting as they had under the old regime.

So there is no either–or. Both to remember and to forget are intrinsic to the law. Law requires perpetrators to be answerable for their guilt; their punishment is a signal showing that something like that must not happen again, and that it will not be accepted but actively opposed. Simultaneously, after a certain amount of time has passed, the law calls for past events to be brought to conclusion and let go. The rule of law also demands closure and settlement if an act was legal at the time it was committed.

The law's ability to be moulded into opposing functions to support the social task of remembering and forgetting is not merely instrumental. However the law is instrumentalised – it shows one of its true functions. Also, it brings the law into conflict with its opposing function. Coming to terms with both the national socialist and communist German past through law created legal conflicts concerning the statute of limitations and the prohibition against retroactive punishment. The time granted under the statute of limitations for prosecution and adjudication of national socialist and communist offences had run out or was about to run out, and, moreover, under the prohibition against retroactive punishment the defendants could only be prosecuted and sentenced if their acts had already been criminal offences at the time.

When the statute of limitations threatened to run out in the sixties and seventies for national socialist offences, and in the nineties for communist ones, extending or suspending the not-yet-expired period of limitations averted the deadlines. Some German legal scholars expressed concern about making such changes in the law governing the statute of limitations. They argued that the prohibition against retroactive punishment would be violated. But the Federal Constitutional Court accepted the extension or suspension of the statutes of limitation that were to expire as in accordance with the constitution. Indeed, there is a lot to be said for punishable acts being defined in law before the deed so that the definition of the crime includes the elements of the offence and its punitive sanctions, but not the duration of the possibility of criminal prosecution. Citizens should feel secure and know which of their behaviours and omissions are punishable and how they will be punished, but they do not have the same need to know how long after the crime the administration of justice will still prosecute them. This also corresponds to the principle of guilt: a citizen does not bring guilt upon themself if they consider their behaviour not to be punishable and, in view of existing law, can believe so in good faith; but they are no less guilty solely because after a set date ensured by law their punishable behaviour will no longer be prosecuted.

More problematic by far under the rule of law is the prosecution and adjudication of national socialist and communist offences that, without a doubt, would never have been prosecuted or punished in the Third Reich or in the GDR. The perpetrator assumed at the time that their behaviour was not punishable, and they could reasonably do so in view of then-existing law. In the Third Reich, when soldiers had murdered Jews without a command to do so and were called into account for their actions before the law, it was for failing to follow the military code and expressly not because of killing Jews; even though murder was, of course, punishable, for soldiers there was an exception and justification for killing Jews. In the GDR, when an attempted illegal border crossing was prevented by firing lethal shots it was justified by the border law of the time and was not only not punished, but praised and rewarded.

The Federal Republic of Germany enshrined in its constitution the prohibition against retroactive punishment, in direct opposition to the statute of the International Military Tribunal in Nuremberg and Allied Forces' Control Council Act Number 10 that expressly suspended it. But from early on, its courts built on a principle articulated by the German legal philosopher Gustav Radbruch in justifying the punishment of national socialist offences. The so-called Radbruch formula states that when statutory law stands in unbearable contradiction to justice, the law must yield and justice be fulfilled. The courts punished the killing of Jews and other offences in accordance with the criminal laws valid during the Third Reich, but by applying the Radbruch formula they stripped the laws of those justifications and exemptions that would have prevented the perpetrators from being punished during the Third Reich. Although the will and command of the Führer was the supreme law and even its sole source under the national socialist system, Hitler's order to annihilate the Jews was, with Radbruch, seen as unable to overcome the essential core of the law, that includes in accordance with the consensus of civilised human beings, the prohibition of genocide.

In dealing with the laws of the GDR, the court decisions of the Federal Republic make a similar argument. Under the aegis of the Radbruch formula, the GDR's legal justifications for fatal shootings at the Wall are ignored because they violate the commonly-held conviction of all people concerning the worth and dignity of human beings and they infringe upon the fundamental idea of humanity and justice. Aside from that, in their decisions the judges considering what the law in the GDR was at the time of the offence did not feel bound by how the law of the GDR was interpreted and applied. Instead, they interpreted the GDR laws as if they were the laws of a constitutional state respecting human rights and the principles of proportionality. Under this Federal Republican interpretation, the GDR's border law could not be interpreted to justify fatal shootings at the Wall.

The idea that GDR laws can be applied according to some later Federal Republican interpretation and are still GDR laws is an attempt to leave the natural law argument of the Radbruch formula behind – natural law is a dubious argument among modern lawyers. But to pit what should and ought to be valid against strict adherence to valid statutory law is true to the spirit of natural law. No reasonable concept of legal validity is yielded when a law's validity at a certain time and place is content free – with the content being filled in in different ways by different later interpretations and applications. There is no way around it: what German courts did, and still do, in dealing with the Third Reich as well as the GDR is use natural law to relativise, to partly neutralise the prohibition against retroactive justice.

When the prohibition against retroactive punishment is valid and enforced, a society can no longer fall back on the stark measures of criminal law statutes to exclude perpetrators from their midst. Instead, integration into the collective biography must be achieved through other means and the fact that exclusion through criminal law cannot be successful must also be integrated. How is this to be done, if a society neither can nor wants to? Or if the past is so horrible that it can only be integrated through the means of criminal law exclusion?

The prohibition against retroactive punishment is guaranteed in nearly all constitutional law countries by their respective constitutions. Therefore, the legislature cannot suspend or alter it through regular legislation. But the legislature has the power to amend the constitution on this point. The relativisation of the prohibition against retroactive punishment achieved by case law at the cost of the integrity of the prohibition would have been attained without this price had an amendment to the constitution suspended the prohibition against retroactive punishment expressly for prosecuting national socialist or communist offences.

Rather than the courts, the legislature would have been answerable for the question of retroactive punishment – with all the political debate and publicity that constitution-amending legislation enjoys. It would have also rightly deserved this discussion and publicity; whether past events should be retroactively punished and thereby excluded or if they should be integrated in another way into the collective biography is one of the critical questions of coming to terms with the past.

There are several grounds for why the leading cases in the Federal Republic answered the question on their own rather than leaving it to the legislative process. For one thing, the crimes of the Third Reich were so heinous that there appeared to be only one possible answer to the question of retroactive punishment; it seemed legally superfluous that this question first be referred to parliament instead of immediately answered by the courts that had to determine the final result concerning retroactive punishment anyway. Second, the old theory of comparative totalitarianism equating national socialism and communism may have played a role in judging the communist past with the same legal tools as the national socialist past. But much more relevant was the simple circumstance that once the GDR offences came up, the criminal law provision against retroactive punishment had already been relativised. The courts were not particularly interested in comparing equal, similar or differing totalitarian political systems and their equal, similar or differing qualities as countries without adequate justice. They needed to consider discrete acts and they found the old jurisprudence on national socialist offences could be applied to GDR offences with some minor adjustments despite the criminal law provision against retroactive punishment. So apply it they did.

Therefore, constitutional debates, discussions and decisions about using constitutional law to come to terms with the national socialist and communist past through retroactive punishment did not take place. The law could not make its most profound contribution in coming to terms with the past. With the constitutional law guarantee against retroactive punishment, the constitution stands as the level at which the question of coming to terms with the past through retroactive punishment is to be asked and answered, as a political question of vital importance, to be answered in a political debate with political publicity to reach political clarification. Surely, it was a lost opportunity for the Federal Republic of Germany that the question was not asked and answered in that manner in coming to terms with the past.

The law's most profound contribution in coming to terms with the past is not what society decides to construct as its past and to integrate into its biography, but how the decisions take place. Somehow the law plays an important role whatever society decides; it supports forgetting in repressive cultures and remembering in cultures of remembrance. But its real work is providing forms and procedures in which decisions about construction and integration are made. It allows for condemning perpetrators not through revolutionary fury and revenge but only through trials, it accepts trials not as irregular revolutionary tribunals but only as regular court cases, it demands that courts decide their cases not through a usurpation of power, but with respect for the law and the decisions of the legislature, it requires decisions of the legislature not with a simple majority but with a qualified constitutional majority once the constitution is at stake, decisions with the corresponding political discussions, publicity and elucidation. In coming to terms with the past, the law's specific contributions are the forms and procedures it provides. They are its contributions to coming to terms with the past and to political culture in general.

Forgiveness and Reconciliation

When I was a child my day ended with a prayer. Before my mother gave me a goodnight kiss, she watched over me as I thanked God for the good things that had happened to me during the day, as I confessed my failings and promised to improve, as I talked about what I had planned for the next day, as I asked for His guidance, and as I prayed for His mercy on those I knew to be sick or in distress. On the nights there weren't too many offerings of thanks, confessions, reports, and requests, I closed the prayer with an 'Our Father'.

One evening I asked God to forgive me for hurting my brother or one of my sisters. After the prayer my mother wanted to know if I had asked for forgiveness from the brother or sister themselves. No, I had not done that. She replied that then I had no right to ask God for forgiveness and that God does not grant forgiveness as long as we have not sought it from those we have injured. We can ask God for forgiveness, she continued, only after our attempt has failed because the other person is too hurt, stubborn or self-righteous to forgive, or if they are dead and can no longer forgive. It sounded to me as if God did not even have the right to forgive as long as the person injured had not exercised their right either to grant or withhold forgiveness.

That is not what my religious mother would have meant, but she certainly believed that the grace of God consists of removing the burden of guilt by forgiving it when we cannot attain forgiveness from those whom we have hurt. For that we need God; that is what He is there for. Or, those who do not believe might point out, mockingly or enviously, that is why those who believe in God invented Him.

I think that my mother was right. If a person does not believe in a forgiving God, then they have to live with their guilt when they can no longer obtain forgiveness from the person they injured. No one can step in as a replacement for the victim to offer forgiveness; forgiveness granted by someone other than the victim is presumptuous. In seeking forgiveness, there is the possibility of advocacy or intercession, but not of stepping in as a replacement. Asking for forgiveness requires the perpetrator to acknowledge that they committed the act that harmed the victim, to affirm their own guilt, and to also recognise the right of the victim to grant or to deny forgiveness – to lift the burden of guilt from the perpetrator or to leave them carrying it. No one can achieve that in the victim's stead.

But often there are more involved than the perpetrator, the victim, and perhaps God. Friends and relatives suffer as well under the effects of the crime, in addition to the actual victim. The trauma suffered by parents can be passed down to children and even grandchildren – as can the guilt.

If an act affects not just the victim, but also the victim's partner, parents, and children, then these affected persons, while not capable of offering forgiveness for what the perpetrator did to the victim, can either grant or withhold forgiveness when the perpetrator seeks it for the suffering they themselves have endured. If the subsequent generation is partially mired in the perpetrator's guilt and partially entangled in the victim's fate, then there is a certain correspondence between the trauma experienced by the victim's children and the burden of guilt carried by the perpetrators' children. The children bound in their parents' fate as victims and those entangled in their parent's guilt as perpetrators belong to the same generation and are connected by the same crime. But the perpetrator's children cannot ask for forgiveness for this crime, and neither can the victim's children grant it. They are not each other's victims or perpetrators.

A young German, grandchild of an SS soldier who was assigned to a concentration camp, one day becomes aware of what his beloved grandfather did and then resolves to make amends and a sign of atonement by working in a kibbutz. He cannot hope for forgiveness when he meets a Jewish boy there who is the grandchild of a man who died in a concentration camp. Loving his grandfather and not breaking off his relationship with him are nothing he did as an affront to the young Jew and nothing for which he could beg him for forgiveness. Correspondingly, the Jewish boy, traumatised by the victimisation of his grandfather in a concentration camp, can neither accuse the young German of it, nor forgive him for it. And yet, the correspondence based on the penumbra of guilt and the fate of the victim makes it understandable that these two young people are able to experience themselves as also being somehow intertwined, as two who have something to talk about and work out.

If entanglement comes to an end by the third or fourth generation, then the relationship between the descendants of the perpetrators and the descendants of the victims becomes more relaxed. But even after generations, it is a common notion that forgiveness must be sought, forgiveness especially for the injustices caused by imperial and colonial oppression, exploitation, enslavement, and murder. Namibia requests that Germany seek its pardon for the brutality with which the Germans suppressed the Herero uprising a hundred years ago. The Herero argue convincingly that the massacre had a permanent and irrevocable impact on their tribe. But such imprints on history are always permanent and irrevocable. The guilt of the Germans who brutally suppressed the revolt died with them long ago, and their children and grandchildren who were bound in guilt with them are also long dead. The request that the Germans of today seek forgiveness from members of the Herero tribe living today calls for an empty ritual that would show little respect for the Herero of that time. Their fight against a brutal German enemy, their heroic defeat, and their pain and suffering are all a part of their identity and dignity. It was their right and theirs alone to define their identity and dignity with clemency or resentment, condemnation or forgiveness. No one else can lay claim to that right, not even his or her descendants.

Forgiveness is something too crucial, too existential to be made into a political ritual or used as an opportunity for politicians to present themselves publicly as deeply moved and with anguished miens. A minister of the interior who seeks forgiveness for the damages the soccer fans of his country have caused in another country, a cardinal who seeks forgiveness for the suffering that the priests under his watch have inflicted on the children entrusted to their care, a chief of police who seeks forgiveness for the brutality employed by his officers on duty – they all ring hollow. Perhaps the police chief did not supervise his officers properly, the cardinal did not pay attention to the complaints lodged by children and parents, and the minister of the interior neglected the problems with rioting football fans. Then they are themselves guilty. If they would seek forgiveness for their own guilt it would have weight; to ask for forgiveness for someone else's guilt is cheap.

My impression is that German politicians are reluctant to ask for forgiveness from Namibia not so much because it would be an empty ritual but rather because Namibia might take it as a title under which it could then claim restitution. I have heard other German politicians take a different position; asking for forgiveness and having it granted would, while unable to create a legal title, give Germany's substantial help for Namibia's development a different aura, an aura of bonding and commitment instead of economic technicality. I don't know about Namibia's intentions; maybe to get if not a legal then at least a quasi-legal title is precisely why Namibia requests that Germany seeks its forgiveness. As much as I can understand all these strategic and tactical considerations, I find forgiveness too existential to be asked for or granted as a strategic or tactical move in negotiations and contracts for restitution.

The right to withhold or grant forgiveness is the victim's right alone as part of their relationship to the perpetrator. Whatever the victim does not forgive cannot be dispensed with through forgiveness by any other family member, descendant, friend, or, especially, politician. The burden remains on the perpetrator and those who are entangled with them in their guilt. The world is full of guilt that has never been forgiven and which can now no longer be forgiven – unless by God.

But forgiveness is not the only response to an injury that keeps it from festering and allows it to rest. Injuries can be condemned, forgotten, and have their burdensome meaning lifted through reconciliation. How forgiveness and reconciliation are similar but also different becomes apparent when we look at those who can forgive and condemn, forget and reconcile.

While only the victim can forgive, anyone can condemn. Anyone includes the victim, though that person may well be too dismayed and overwhelmed by the event to pass judgment concerning the perpetrator impartially. But to pass judgment means both to identify the crime and the perpetrator, and the determination of just punishment. While the victim may not be capable of determining just punishment, he can certainly charge the perpetrator with the crime.

Everyone is also capable of forgetting. On occasion someone is too deeply injured to ever forget the injury. But again and again one observes someone who is so grievously injured that no one believes they could ever be capable of forgetting who finally does forget.

Just as one can lose the ability to judge impartially when one is in shock or has a conflict of interest, and as one can lose the ability to forget when one is particularly seriously injured, one can also lose the right to pass judgment or to forget. Those who live in a glass houses shouldn't throw stones – whoever has some guilt to contend with should not go around accusing and judging others. Certainly, under the rule of law if a charge is true, then it is true regardless of who made it – it can even be someone who also deserves to be accused and judged. But while this person may still have the right to accuse and judge, they have lost the credibility to do so. Their right to accuse and to judge and to condemn is not accepted unless they ensure that they recognise the precarious nature of the charge coming out of their mouth and explain why they are making it anyway. Similarly, when someone claims that they have forgotten about the crime they committed they will not be entitled to their forgetfulness, and here not even assurances and explanations will help. How can the perpetrator allow themself to forget what they have done – the reaction is speechlessness and indignation. Forgetting can make forgiving easier for the victim, but the perpetrator should not be allowed to make it easier on themself. To forget and pass judgment are the rights of others.

The circle of participants is again small when it comes to reconciliation. In the history of this concept it was not always the case; in German the term *Versöhnung* (reconciliation), was originally related to the term *Verurteilen* (to pass judgment). It included attributing the deed to the perpetrator and determining the atonement required of them in order to stave off revenge and restore public order. As atonement imposed by the legal community developed into the state-regulated system of compensation for damages on the one hand, and the system of state-imposed and -executed punishments on the other, reconciliation became a concept defined as the restoration of peace between people explicitly without state sanctions. After the end of Apartheid, as South Africa strived for truth and reconciliation, it did not want the state to sentence and punish, exclude and lock away. Instead the goal was to heal the damaged relationships between the perpetrators and victims through institutionalised, moderated encounters in such a way that they could once more live side by side with each other.

More people than just the perpetrators and victims can be involved in reconciling with each other. The children and grandchildren who share the perpetrator's guilt and the victim's fate can reconcile, enemies can reconcile who are simultaneously perpetrators and victims, even friends and lovers who fought and perhaps only inadvertently injured or wronged or lost each other can reconcile – simply stated, everyone whose relationships have been damaged can reconcile. While forgiveness lifts the burden of guilt from the guilty parties, reconciliation merely makes it a bit lighter. Reconciliation means that further attempts to coexist should no longer fail on account of guilt and recriminations.

At the very least, reconciliation calls for the recognition that others are human beings like ourselves, and for the insight that this equality must sometimes be sufficient to establish the foundation for living together in peace. Sometimes those seeking reconciliation can build on a broader foundation for their coexistence. Then political parties form unusual coalitions mindful of their common responsibility for the delicate state of their country – as happened in most countries at the beginning of the First World War, and in the United States when the country was made to believe that Saddam Hussein was a serious threat because he had weapons of mass destruction. Catholics and Protestants sometimes remember that more than anything else they are both Christians and celebrate the Eucharist together – it happens in hostile territory, between soldiers and prisoners of war in camps. Quarrelling lovers sometimes call to mind that their love is greater than their fight. Against all that would separate us, reconciliation emphasises the ties that bind, from equality to love.

Reconciliation requires at least two people. A third party can reconcile two people whose relationship with each other has been damaged, and there can be not just two but many who repair their damaged relationships by reconciling or being reconciled with each other. Someone may be too gravely injured to reconcile, or they may only be ready to reconcile if judgment or forgiveness has preceded it. But whenever two are ready to reconcile with each other there is no reason to argue against their ability or right to do so. When, however, politicians celebrate reconciliation as if they could heal not only their own damaged relationships but also those between peoples and parties with their embraces, it must be insisted upon vis-à-vis this pretension that reconciliation can only happen directly between those whose relationships with each other are damaged. Not even the Nobel Prize helps; when Briand and Stresemann got it, France and Germany were still not ready for reconciliation, nor were the USA and Vietnam when Kissinger and Le Duc Tho were awarded or the Israelis and the Palestinians when the prize went to Arafat, Peres and Rabin. With reconciliation there is just as little proxy as with forgiveness.

If truth and reconciliation are the goals, then truth is the prerequisite for reconciliation. In the South African Truth and Reconciliation Commissions the perpetrators were supposed to genuinely confess their deeds to the victims if they did not want to have their amnesty stripped from them – a threat that was seldom enforced against the perpetrators, just as the promised reparations for the victims seldom came through. If there was any success at all to awaken a readiness to reconcile between the participants it was not due simply to truth. Reconciliation succeeded when the perpetrator presented him- or herself genuinely, listened and provided answers, withstood the victims' outpouring of emotion and did not hide their own feelings. In order to acknowledge the perpetrator as an equal and to reconcile with them, the victim has to understand the perpetrator, even if they can understand them only in disbelief or in disapproval. Reconciliation requires a truth that can be understood; it requires understanding.

That is not the case with forgiving and condemning – and it is obvious that forgetting and understanding are not compatible. Whoever wants to forgive someone is free to understand or not to understand them; the victim does not owe the other person any understanding. Forgiveness may help them make peace with themself more than with the other person with whom they finally wish to reach closure but without getting involved or understanding. Condemning also works without understanding: in earlier legal systems knowledge that the perpetrator committed the deed sufficed for judgment to be made against them, and today the law only requires knowledge that the deed was committed knowingly and intentionally, or sometimes negligently.

This is not to say that understanding is completely unrelated to condemning and forgiving. The more one understands, the more one is enticed into forgiveness and led away from passing judgment. A verdict without an understanding of the perpetrator, their circumstances, motivations, and limitations is not easily accepted today as a just verdict. Such understanding connotes insight, particularly into the causes of the deed that were outside the perpetrator's control, and it becomes increasingly difficult to pass judgment against the perpetrator for the deed as an expression of their own free will. That is what is meant by the aphorism '*tout comprendre c'est tout pardoner*'. It has an even deeper meaning, since true understanding is more than searching for and finding causes. It includes putting yourself in someone else's place, putting yourself into someone else's thoughts and someone else's feelings and seeing the world through that person's eyes. How then could you condemn the other, how could you not forgive, if you empathise with them on that level?

Thus, understanding does not have only positive connotations. The aphorism is often quoted with ironic condescension and as a warning: whoever thinks and feels understandingly is giving up the distance needed to make dispassionate assessments and clear decisions; he or she gets caught up in the mire of forgiving indecisiveness and permissiveness and becomes unsuited to the necessary harshness of condemning. Condescension and irony aside – tension necessarily arises for those who want to understand the perpetrator in his or her crime. The tension exists especially for the perpetrator's children and grandchildren; they know that their parents and grandparents should be condemned but they still love them too much, know them too well, not to want to understand them and, in their understanding, they tend towards clemency. Between wanting to understand and having to condemn they can find no really workable course of behaviour. It is as if understanding would contaminate the pure business of forgiving and condemning, and it begs the question of whether it does not discredit itself as a precondition for reconciliation.

But understanding's weakness is exactly its strength. Connecting ourselves with the thoughts and feelings of others, although they may be completely different than ours, establishes equality; just as interpreting their rationality in the light of our own, despite major differences, creates parity. Understanding allows us to see that we are equal with others and can experience, empathise and share in their rationality, empirical and normative expectations, thoughts and feelings. We make them equal to us and us to them; we build up society when we understand. Since understanding makes us more hesitant to pass judgment and more forbearing and tending toward forgiveness, understanding brings reconciliation a step closer. The foundation for reconciliation is laid by understanding because it works against all that separates us and toward all that would bring us together.

The ground can slide away and attempts at reconciliation can collapse. While forgiving and condemning settle the consequences of a deed once and for all, and forgetting a crime settles it with the proviso that what has been forgotten can also be remembered again, reconciliation heals only as well and persists only as long as the participants understand each other and acknowledge each other as equals. When the effort at mutual understanding becomes too much for them, if an old injury remains a current source of pain or if it resurfaces through an accidental or a provoked event, or if an outside pressure to acknowledge the other as an equal falls away, then reconciliation again can fail – between peoples, within societies, and in relationships.

This is the problem of reconciliation based only on truth and understanding that forgoes the power of closure that condemning and forgiving offer. The work of the South African Truth and Reconciliation Commissions was often regarded with some scepticism because it was not flanked by judgments against the perpetrators who refused to cooperate and by restitution for the victims. To be sure, restitution does not have the power of closure like forgiveness, but it contains a request for forgiveness and makes forgiveness easier to grant.

Passing judgment does not necessarily have to be pursued through legal proceedings in a court of law in order for it to safeguard and stabilise reconciliation through its powers of closure. But without identification of the deed and its perpetrator, without a determination of guilt and imposition of some sort of sanction, without all of this happening publicly, visibly, and through an agency with real authority, it is difficult to reach closure. If passing judgment and restitution are unavailable options, then forgetting can still help and reconciliation means freedom from the wreckage of the past, allowing it to be both remembered and forgotten. But forgetting is not a reliable helper.

Restitution often goes hand in hand with rituals, condemning always does. Reconciliation, too, recognises rituals and icons and it probably needs them. When orchestras from one country perform in another, paintings from one country's museums are exhibited in another's country, or partnership and exchange programs are arranged, these exchanges promote mutual understanding and they are also attempts to solidify reconciliation through public ritual.

Politicians who stand hand in hand at a memorial site or lay down a wreath in a cemetery are trying to tangibly express reconciliation, and sometimes they succeed: the picture of Willy Brandt kneeling in Warsaw became an iconic image of reconciliation.

Forgiving, condemning, forgetting and reconciliation – of all the ways to achieve closure in the wake of an injury, reconciliation is the most demanding and difficult. Often enough, that is the very reason why it does not happen. The German experience shows, however, that when it is seriously undertaken it has a good chance of succeeding. A resurgence of the old hostility between France and Germany is unimaginable, and it is unimaginable between Poland and Germany, although the efforts at reconciliation were less intensive and hence the positive results of reconciliation are less evident. Between Jews and Germans there is every indication that in a few generations they will no longer meet harbouring old prejudices, though they may still regard each other with special interest. Studies and questionnaires sometimes indicate that the rift between East and West Germans remains deep and is even getting deeper. Reconciliation was never seriously attempted in this case. It was not really even perceived as a necessary exercise; the thought was that under the roof of common institutions the damages in the relationship would heal on their own. But only forgetting functions on its own; it has its own dynamic and follows its own course. Forgiving and condemning become superfluous when the perpetrators are dead. The degree to which reconciliation occurs depends on the level of efforts made to achieve it. Reconciliation is an endeavour for the long term.

Prudence and Corruption

1970 was a year that divided two different political climates. In the sixties, foreign affairs were full of conflict and tension, but there was much hope in domestic affairs. The sixties saw the construction of the Berlin Wall, the Cuban missile crisis, and the escalation of the war in Vietnam. At the same time, they saw Kennedy's New Frontier and Johnson's Great Society in the US, liberal, social democratic and socialist governments replaced conservative administrations across Europe, and on both sides of the Atlantic students protested against rigid institutions and for peace and the power of love. In the seventies the situation was reversed; the years brought the end to the Vietnam War, détente between East and West, and an easing of tension in the Near East, but domestically conflicts intensified; peaceful student protests descended into violent demonstrations and were met with an increase of government repression, each feeding off the other.

Of course, the major shift between the sixties and seventies did not happen all in one year. In 1970, however, there were events that symbolically presaged it: the National Guard was sent in against demonstrators at Kent State University, Ulrike Meinhof helped Andreas Baader escape from prison, starting the terrorist Baader-Meinhof group, Willy Brandt kneeled at the Memorial of the Warsaw Ghetto Uprising. Just as pressure built up by gradual tectonic movement is suddenly released in earthquakes, the change in political climate erupted in a storm of demonstrations.

In 1970, young people took to the streets all over the world, as if a better world could be found there. In Germany, they demonstrated against the American engagement in Vietnam and Cambodia, for the students shot down at Kent State University, against Apartheid in South Africa, against the construction of the Cabora-Bassa Dam in Mozambique, for the workers shot in Gdansk, out of joy over Lenin's one-hundredth birthday and Allende's election victory, out of sadness for the deaths of Jimi Hendrix and Janis Joplin, for reform in the universities and education system, for cheaper public transportation, against the strengthening National Democratic Party, in Frankfurt for a better police, in Dortmund for the mini-skirt. They demonstrated with serious purpose or as a joke, militantly or playfully, often with absurd overestimation of their significance and sometimes even with ironic distance to themselves.

On 19 June 1970 there was an international conference on development policy strategies in my hometown Heidelberg and the President of the World Bank, Robert S McNamara, participated. The students of the SDS, the Socialist Union of German Students, were outraged; in their eyes development policy strategies were capitalistic and imperialistic, and the presence of the one-time American Secretary of Defense was a provocation. They organised a demonstration that was supposed to 'break up' the conference, and the police prepared themselves for a violent confrontation. As some of the demonstrators tried to storm the Hotel Europäischer Hof where the conference was being held and were driven back by the police, a street battle ensued during which demonstrators pelted the police with paint bombs, wooden slats and stones and the police countered with water cannons, tear gas and truncheons. There were injured demonstrators and injured police officers, several students were taken into custody for a short time, and a member of the SDS was charged with attempted manslaughter for having hurled a piece of iron at a police officer. He was taken to prison, which led to further demonstrations and to further use of tear gas. Naturally, the students and the police disputed the details of what actually happened and who was responsible for the escalation of violence. But it was indisputable that the violence on either side had escalated in a way Heidelberg had not seen before – even though all the injuries were treatable on an outpatient basis and the charge of attempted manslaughter was soon dropped.

Across the street from the Hotel Europäischer Hof is the University of Heidelberg's law school. On 19 June its doors were carefully supervised; it was not supposed to be affected by any street battles. When two young female students sought entry they were reluctantly let in. One, an education major, had been beaten by the police, lost her glasses, was distraught and crying; she was brought into the law school by the other student, a law student, so she could freshen up and calm herself down. As they both came out of the restroom and wanted to leave the building, they found the doors were locked and Professor S wanted to know who they were. The law student gave her name and semester. But why did he ask? The education student snapped that he should keep his mouth shut and let them get out. Did she also call him a 'filthy pig' as Professor S reported to the Heidelberg press? In any case, he slapped her across the face and then, according to the students' report, he became enraged and struck the education student again and again. According to Professor S's report both students left the law school without further incident after the slap.

There was no legal consequence to the incident; the district attorney's investigation against the professor was dropped and an investigation against the education student was never opened. But there was a consequence of a different kind. On 22 June, the law students held a plenary meeting in response to the events of 19 June. Not all the law students were gathered but the politically active ones were there, especially those from the Basis Gruppe Jura, the association of radical-left law students at Heidelberg University in those days. They resolved that 'S no longer lecture'. A professor hit a student – the students did not want to let him get away with it. And they especially did not want to let this particular professor get away with it since in previous years he had attacked the students' representation for their political position and had refused the Basis Gruppe the use of law school rooms that other student groups had enjoyed. He had fought them politically, using the law as a weapon while simultaneously preaching the apolitical formality and neutrality of the law. And in 1938, he had recognised the will and command of the Führer as the source of all law.

On the 24 June, shortly after 8 am, the yard in front of the main university building was crowded with students as Professor S tried to enter to teach his class. Most of the students wanted to prevent him from going in, but there were also some who wanted to procure his entrance. One of his colleagues and several assistants accompanied him to offer him their support and to witness everything that happened, and the vice rector of the university was at the ready to diffuse the conflict and to guarantee that the class could take place. The stage was set for the usual drama of the time: an exchange of indignant and enraged words, screaming and tussling and, at the end, the professor's retreat, or, perhaps arbitrated by the vice president, the students' exit. But instead of this little political mini-drama, a personal vendetta was performed. A friend of the student who had been slapped, a chemistry major, sprayed Professor S from behind with a rancid liquid. The stench was intense, the students were aghast, and the professor feared chemical burns and other injuries. That was it for the class and the blockade; the professor let himself be taken to the hospital and the students dispersed.

The liquid turned out to be butyric acid, non-corrosive, non-injurious and only foul smelling. But in the portrayals that followed, the event gained a more and more dangerous timbre. The faculty of the law school stated that Professor S 'was forced to submit himself for medical treatment', he himself insisted that he was 'injured', and a magazine reported that 'suddenly the professor felt a horrible burning sensation on his back. He doubled over in pain.' Everyone waited for the official statement of the attending physician, a professor in the medical school; he chose to remain silent citing the doctor–patient privilege of confidentiality.

One of the students who wanted to block Professor S's entrance to the university on 24 June was Volker N. Professor S and other professors later accused him of being the 'ringleader' of the Basis Gruppe and of 'plotting' the blockade.

But the Basis Gruppe was a loose association of students without official members and official leaders and the blockade had been planned at a plenary meeting. Yet among the members and supporters of that group, Volker N was certainly the most theoretically advanced and the most articulate.

I got to know him as an interesting opponent in seminars and then later when we sometimes met privately to spar over questions of state and constitutional legal theory, about the role of law and the use of force and about the writings of Carl Schmitt and Walter Benjamin. I was a law clerk and not a student any more, but still attended some seminars at the university and in the law school. For the left-leaning students I was a 'damned liberal', meaning one of those who recognised the necessity of reform but who accepted the political and economic system and put faith in the law to solve problems equitably. I rejected violence and also forcing discussions in the middle of lectures, blockading them and disrupting them. But I was also appalled by the legal aggressiveness that the law school professors used to fight against everything that did not suit them politically. They found the political mandate of the students' representation legally acceptable as long as the students took positions that were against communism, in favor of a unified Germany and European unification. But they were not above exploiting the law to resist the students when their opinions were against the Vietnam War or in favour of governmental and societal reforms. As the students became more radical, the professors regarded themselves as increasingly surrounded by enemies against whom they could only win or lose. They had lost their confidence in the reflective and constructive strengths of the university, and instead relied on the state and the police.

The student movement came to an end in the early seventies, in the middle of the eighties it became the subject matter of historical study, and by the early nineties it was only a distant, weak memory. Heidelberg had long since returned to being the peaceful, pretty university town it had been at the beginning of the student movement. Germany was no longer divided or subject to the tensions of straddling

East and West. We know today that the world did not see a reduction in political tensions and catastrophes at the end of the Cold War. But in the early years of the nineties it seemed for a while as if it had and as if most of its problems could be solved through diplomacy and law enforcement.

In the meantime Professor S, along with most of the other professors who had been at the centre of the conflict in 1970, had become professor emeritus. Volker N passed his first and second state exam, wrote a doctorate, started a career as a lecturer, and at the end of 1991 completed his habilitation in public law at the law school of the University of Frankfurt. I was teaching at the University of Frankfurt at the time and, along with my Frankfurt colleagues, I signed the recommendation to admit Private Lecturer Dr Volker N to the Association of German Constitutional Law Professors.

The association, founded in 1922, disbanded in 1938, and re-established in 1949, is the leading organisation for German constitutional and administrative law academicians. Practically all professors and private lecturers who teach public law at German, Austrian and German-speaking Swiss universities are members of it. Whoever is not recommended for membership, or is not accepted despite recommendation, suffers long-term damage to, if not complete ruin of, his or her career. To be invited to make a presentation and to give a decent presentation at an annual conference are crucial steps for one's career. The topics of the presentations, sometimes more political, sometimes more doctrinal and practical, sometimes more theoretical, reflect what the association and often the society are concerned about at the moment. The presentations are conservative rather than innovative in tone, and this corresponds to the conservative undertone of German public law academicians. Indeed, lawyers never march at the forefront of change. An appreciation for tradition and its power to keep order and stabilise is inherent in the teachers of public law as well as in those who teach civil and criminal law. Constitutional and administrative jurisprudence is, however, traditionally especially conservative. Jurisdiction in matters of constitutional and administrative law was created substantially later than jurisdiction in civil or criminal law. Fighting in court over matters of administrative law only came in the late ninteenth century, and over matters of constitutional law in the mid twentieth century, while in other areas of the law it has been common since the middle ages. Therefore, in the exchange of ideas between academia and practice, in civil and criminal law, the academic has always had, besides the judge, the conflict-happy practising attorney as their partner. In public law the academic's partner was and prominently still is the conflict-averse civil servant whose concern is the smooth functioning of the state and its government and administration.

The by-laws of the Association of German Constitutional Law Professors regulate admittance. The process is commenced through written recommendation of at least three members. Thereupon, the executive committee offers membership to the recommended scholar, except if there are doubts about whether the membership requirements have been fulfilled, or if at least five members raise an objection or request an oral debate concerning acceptance.

The debate then takes place at the annual membership meeting.

There were forty-nine objections or motions for oral debate filed with the executive committee in response to the recommendation signed by eight of the Frankfurt members to accept Volker N for membership. This was an astoundingly large number of members who became active against Volker N's admittance. There had never been anything like it.

Professor S and the colleague who had accompanied him at that time on the way to class raised the first two objections. Their objections described the blockade, stated that Professor S had been 'injured' and an ambulance 'had to be' found. That Professor S had slapped or even beaten a female student beforehand, that the liquid was harmless and that Volker N was no more involved in the blockade than hundreds of other students was not mentioned. Professor S argued that because Volker N could be characterised as a 'conniving political functionary . . . exhibiting consistent ruthlessness [and] cold recklessness', who 'had practised illegal uses of force against members of the association' and had 'violently fought against the academic freedom to teach' he would be 'intolerable' as a member.

The objections that followed sometimes employed even stronger language. What Volker N had done, one said, would imply 'a fundamental negation of our constitutional law', and whoever acts as he did would place himself 'outside every civilised society and is especially incapable of taking part in the scholarly pursuit of law'. Some threatened to withdraw their membership if Volker N were allowed in. Several tried to build bridges, suggesting that Volker N could be accepted if he apologised to Professor S. Naturally, some made the lawyer's favourite motion for when matters get difficult: the decision should be deferred. Only a few letters to the executive committee expressed their support in favour of Volker N's acceptance. The executive committee itself did not take a position.

The cards were dealt. The annual conference of the Association of German Constitutional Law Professors took place in October 1992 in Bayreuth and commenced, as always, with the afternoon membership meeting. The room filled up quickly with 165 members, the chairman opened the meeting and the debate began. It did not go well. Many who had submitted letters of objection again called for the rejection of Volker N's acceptance. They were not only more numerous than those who spoke up for his acceptance, they also received the stronger applause. I looked around: even the younger colleagues were applauding the older ones who were talking once again about the attack on academic freedom to teach, criticising the lack of an apology in the meantime, or saying it would be too much for Professor S to be in the very same organisation as Volker N.

Those who supported Volker N's admittance referred to the by-laws. The conditions for membership required only 'outstanding academic performance' and activity 'as a researcher and teacher'. Volker N's scholarly works were mentioned wherein nothing blameworthy and nothing hostile to the constitution, democracy and rule of law could be found. The earlier forbearance of the Association of German Constitutional Law Professors, who in the fifties had without problem accepted academicians tainted by national socialism, was recollected. In my own statement I described the situation in Heidelberg in the early seventies as a university-level civil war, and called to mind that a civil war finds its appropriate ending in an amnesty that leaves the questions of law and guilt behind, lets them fall prey to being forgotten and thereby establishes the grounds for a new coexistence.

No one spoke about what actually happened in the summer of 1970. No one mentioned that Professor S had slapped a female student and that the ensuing students' blockade of his class was the students' response to it. No one spoke about the impertinence of bringing up a story more than twenty years old as if there had been no historical context for it, or as if a professor's behaviour were sacrosanct for students, or as if the Association of German Constitutional Law Professors had committed itself to the political position of the objecting professors' generation and would have to continue its political struggles indefinitely. Instead our arguments for admitting Volker N were peaceable and conciliatory. Without having come to any previous agreement, each of his supporters talked about the conflict that erupted after the objections as something really so small that it appeared entirely out of proportion to deny Volker N his acceptance on that account.

Already as I was speaking I did not have a good feeling. At first I thought it was the oppressive atmosphere in the room, the dogmatic airs of Volker N's opponents so certain of their victory, the scant number of his supporters, the strong applause against him, and the meagre clapping that we who supported his admittance received, the hostility visible in some of the faces. But if that is all it had been – then would I not have felt better when we won?

Yes, we won. In a secret ballot Volker N was admitted with eighty-seven ayes and sixty-one nays and seventeen abstentions. The younger colleagues had indeed openly applauded the older ones, their mentors for their doctorate, and their habilitation whose goodwill they depended upon for their careers and which they did not want to lose. But in secret they did not want to have anything to do with the ancient history of their political affairs.

We who had supported Volker N's admittance received a few compliments. How good it was that we led the discussion so diplomatically in this important disagreement. How good it was that the senior members could have lost their fight without losing face over it. How good it was that our younger colleagues could vote against the old ones without disavowing them too severely and laying themselves too open to criticism. How good it was that Volker N was accepted; they would not have believed it could be accomplished. How excellent that the whole nasty business could be settled without tearing the association apart with resignations or any other further offence.

We won and still a thorn in my side remained, and whenever I thought about the fight for Volker N's acceptance in the Association of German Constitutional Law Professors the same bad feeling returned.

Years later I read a doctoral dissertation that one of my research assistants wrote about the law school faculty at the Berlin University in the upheaval of 1933. The situation was critical in the spring of 1933; the law school faculty was largely Jewish, a Jewish dean and assistant dean ran the program. Among the professors there were neither convinced national socialists nor resolved opponents of national socialism, instead there were politically moderately engaged legal scholars, irritated by the change of circumstances, peaceably going forward in their research and teaching. They got hit with pressure from above by the new national socialist Minister of Culture and from below by the national socialists among the students. It was only at the beginning of the summer semester that Jewish professors were forcibly put on leave and a new election for the dean was organised. But already at the beginning of March the dean and the assistant dean of the law school had resigned from their official positions.

It happened quietly. The minutes of the faculty meetings make no note of any removal or resignation from office or new election; at the beginning of March the Jewish dean simply invited everyone to a meeting and a dinner in his apartment, as was customary at the end of a period in office. The next meeting at the end of April was led by an informally appointed new dean. Since this person officiated both as dean and assistant dean, the position held by the Jewish assistant dean was simply made to disappear.

The dissertation explores the reasons behind this pre-emptory rush of obedience and cannot find its origin in national socialist zeal, in anti-Semitic malice, or even out of fear over job security and salary. It appears much more plausible that the Jewish and non-Jewish colleagues agreed to avoid every provocation and escalation. They did not want to provide anyone with a target and chose a response meant to protect Jewish as well as non-Jewish colleagues from attacks. Even later, when leaves-of-absence, firings and other machinations were enforced against Jewish professors, everyone's efforts, those of Jewish and non-Jewish colleagues alike, were directed toward minimising the problems behind the scenes with assistance from old established contacts within the ministry in hopes to solve them through diplomatic channels. Anything not to alienate the Minister, anything not to defy the students!

Over the spring of 1933, the law school faculty allowed itself to be corrupted. It was not corruption on account of a lust for power or money or fame. It was corruption through good intentions. No one wanted the Jewish professors to be exposed to unfavourable treatment. It is true that the non-Jewish professors did not want to be exposed to unfavourable treatment either, but that did not preclude them from simultaneously having good intentions. Corruption through good intentions, just like every other form of corruption, has its price. In 1933, when the diplomatic channels, so often relied upon in the old days, had led nowhere, it was already too late for protests which would have had to have happened earlier, and not just because they had become dangerous in the meantime. Protests would no longer have been credible after the professors had at first accepted the rules as they had been presented to them by the national socialist regime and had attempted to find a solution under the premise of these rules.

The dissertation also documents how the law school faculties in Munich and Cologne supported their Jewish colleagues and defended them against the attacks from the ministry and the students. In the end, they were not successful either. It makes us feel good to read about them today anyway – someone at least set a good example. For the faculty members in Munich and Cologne it was not about setting an example. For them, like the Berliners, it was about success. None of the members of these faculties had predicted their failure – nor could they have. How could the professors of the Berlin law school anticipate that the diplomatic manoeuvres they had so masterfully executed before 1933 would no longer amount to anything after 1933? On the other hand, how could the professors in Munich and Cologne have any idea that their engagement, at first successful, finally would be to no avail? Each one did what their experience trained them to do in their relations with the university and the ministry, and they both acted with good intentions. But the professors of the Berlin University allowed themselves to be corrupted, and one cannot read this story of corruption without finding it disturbing.

And that is why the thorn in my side and the bad feeling remained. I, too, had allowed myself to be corrupted. On account of my good intentions, I, too, had not said what needed to be said about the events in the summer of 1970 and about the unwarranted uproar in the autumn of 1992. I had wanted to help Volker N and not hurt his chances by escalating the conflict, provoking his opponents, and irritating the silent majority. This well-intentioned corruption could easily have exacted its price too, and again the price would have been credibility. Had Volker N's acceptance been rejected, it would have been too late to say what needed to be said in the Association of German Constitutional Law Professors. Those of us in favour of admitting him had allowed ourselves to be drawn into the argument under the terms as the opponents to his admission had defined them and we could no longer have credibly withdrawn from those terms in a second attempt. Certainly, we would have been able to nominate Volker N again for membership, but only with the background and under the consideration that his behaviour as a student had disqualified him in the first round. His acceptance in the second round would have been a mere act of mercy.

We did not have to pay that price. We were lucky and we won. That our diplomatic actions would meet with success was something we could not have foreseen. We also could not have predicted the outcome had we followed another, direct, confrontational and adversarial course of action. Would the members have rejected this course of action and then also Volker N's acceptance? Or would the effect have been to chase away the fears, caution and hesitations that were paralysing the discussion? I must admit that at the time I did not once consider the question. I simply accepted the situation as it had been defined by others.

Today the stories from the autumn of 1992 in Bayreuth and the summer of 1970 in Heidelberg are historic footnotes. Because the past that ended with the autumn of 1992 and the past that began with the spring of 1933 are absolutely incomparable, it appears as though the situations in Bayreuth and in Heidelberg are also of completely different types. The situation in Bayreuth looks minor, inconsequential and harmless and the one in Berlin looms large, and portends doom and danger. But that is the perspective of hindsight. The perspective prior to the events was that there were two minor situations threatening problems, conflicts and frustrations but nothing of a really serious nature. That in 1933 the world would be turned upside down and in 1992 everything remained in good order, that in Berlin the diplomatic, though corrupted, course of action would fail and no amount of luck could help while in Bayreuth luck intervened and diplomacy succeeded – all that was hidden at the time.

Once the consequences of any one action are largely unforeseeable; strategic and tactical calculations can offer no point of reference. So at first what I thought I should learn was that it is proper to simply do the right thing in such situations – to say what needs to be said without regard for diplomacy, but without the risk of corruption. I also thought that I should never again do what I had done in Bayreuth where I accepted the situation as others had defined it for me and did not even think to question the chances of another more direct, confrontational and adversarial course.

Then I started to regard my behaviour in Bayreuth less harshly – as I also judge the Berlin professors' behaviour in a slightly more favourable light. I said to myself that one cannot make things work without accepting situations defined by others. The terms of reality are mostly determined by others and to be successful in the real world we must submit to it as it stands. The success in Bayreuth confirmed that the situation was as the others had defined it and as we had accepted it. I also said to myself that my generation had refused for too long to accept reality and had held on to an unreasonable belief in our ability to create a new reality. In the early seventies we took our exams and started our careers, got married and started families – the years of moral and political zeal, and the naïve belief that the older generation is guilty and principally in the wrong and our young one is innocent and in the right, were over. But it still took a long time until the communist cells and radical sects disbanded, until among the green party a realist minority developed beside its fundamentalist majority, and until diplomacy and compromise were deemed as respectable as confrontation and conflict. From this perspective, the autumn of 1992 in Bayreuth was simply a late chapter in my long departure from an early moralistic railing against the messiness of reality. Still, the moral thorn in my side has never gone away.

Stories about the Past

In the first five essays I talked about perpetrators and victims, about the entanglement of following generations into the perpetrators' guilt and the victims' trauma and about forgiveness and reconciliation. I talked about how the past reaches into the present. In this last essay I would like to talk about present fiction reaching back to the past. Are there rules for fiction dealing with the past? Is it anything goes? There are people who were not heard or not seen and who want their truth acknowledged, traumatised people who want their trauma respected, people deprived of a dignified life who want their dignity restored. Their expectations come to the fore whenever someone writes about the past they experienced. Can these wants be dismissed or must they be honoured?

I think the foremost question is whether fiction has to be true. What is truth in fiction? Is it that the facts that fiction presents happened or at least could have happened? But what if fiction does not claim to present facts? What if the story is clearly a fairytale, a satire, a comedy, which by definition does not limit itself to what happened or could have happened? Are authors allowed to craft fairytales, satires or comedies about anything at all? Even about the Holocaust? Adorno's famous statement from 1951 that to write a poem after Auschwitz is barbarian, (*nach Auschwitz ein Gedicht zu schreiben ist barbarisch*) certainly includes poems about Auschwitz and, to be sure, any Auschwitz comedy or satire. Are there events so serious and awful that they can only be documented, or at best fictionalised so that they present what happened or what could have happened?

I have heard and read affirmation of this position more than once, but I don't think it is meant to be taken literally. After all, a fairy-tale, a satire or a comedy can open one's eyes to truth as effectively as a documentary can; and fiction presenting what happened and only what happened can create a veneer of truth that distorts by omitting what also happened. What lies behind the idea that some events may not be fictionalised or may only be fictionalised while remaining true to the facts is not about the genre, not about documentation versus fiction, not about this kind of fiction versus that kind of fiction. It is about authenticity in a fuller sense.

If I understand correctly, what lies behind the refusal to fictionalise an event such as the Holocaust, or to reject its representation in certain ways or forms, is the fear that the full truth might get lost. It is a fear that truth might disappear not only through the imaginings and fabrications of well- or ill-intentioned authors but also through true but singular and misleading aspects of what happened. Even if there might have been a funny moment in Auschwitz, even if there might have been a decent concentration camp guard, even if there might have been a fairytale element in someone's rescue from persecution and horror – couldn't a novel, a play, a comedy about this make the reader or viewer forget that the full reality was profoundly different? It's understandable how this fear gives way to the demand that an event like the Holocaust should be documented but not fictionalised or only fictionalised in a way that makes the full truth visible. A good documentary can make us understand the full truth – just remember *Shoah* – and fiction is able to do the same; it can capture and represent single moments and episodes in a way that makes us aware of the large picture – just think of Primo Levi's or Imre Kertész's work. And it can fail. I, at least, could not find the whole picture in Benigni's comedic movie *Life is Beautiful* about a Jewish father and his son being deported into a concentration camp where the father manages to present everything to his son as a complicated game with complicated rules that the son has to master to win the prize: an American tank. And I understand the twofold criticism that has been levelled at the film: its myopic perspective and its strange use of comedy were both misleading.

But to turn that fear into a demand for only certain types of representation reveals both too much and too little faith. The demand that artistic representations of the Holocaust be presented so that the whole picture becomes visible shows too little faith in viewers' and readers' ability to create the whole picture for themselves. Now that such a multitude of books and articles, plays and films have come out, whether individual works show only certain aspects of what happened matters much less. The whole picture is present anyway. The demand that the Holocaust not be presented in a comedic or otherwise reductive way, on the other hand, shows too much faith in the power of social norms – excluding any other type of norm for the moment. The norm would not succeed and would even be counterproductive. More than anything else it would trigger the wish to come up with something provoking and scandalising.

Germany and some other countries have a norm against reductive representation of the

Holocaust that is also codified as a legal norm in the penal code that makes Holocaust-denial a criminal offence. The law signifies that our society is united in its willingness to accept its past and deal with it – it is a tangible demonstration of that acceptance addressed at ourselves as well as others. It also somewhat protects Jews for whom the Holocaust has become an integral element of their individual and collective identity. But one unintended effect of the norm is that those who set out to deny the Holocaust don't do it bluntly any more. Rather they minimise what happened in a very skilled and subtle manner. The vice president of my university once gave me a print-out of one of the internet pages that minimise the Holocaust; it had been sent to him anonymously and he had given it to the police. But the police knew it already and couldn't do anything because the denial was too subtle. Instead of any blunt Holocaust denial, it presented and documented facts and asked questions like: the graves of all the great massacres of the last century have been found, from Katyn to Cambodia and Kosovo – why is it that the graves of Jews murdered by Germans found in Eastern Europe don't by far add up to the four million murder victims that are the official number? The graves found at Babi Yar and elsewhere prove that German troops, or rather their local helpers, committed regrettable atrocities but nothing on the scale of the official numbers. I read the internet page with my students and, even though they had been taught extensively about the Holocaust, they found it far from easy to counter its arguments. So here the effect of the norm is not a will to provoke, since a provocation would be punishable, but something else similarly undesirable: a distortion of the truth that is not easy to detect and refute. There is always a social price for norms that limit what one is allowed to say – sometimes the price is worthwhile but, often enough, it's not.

A common version of the demand on fiction to show the whole truth demands that it be representative. So if a book about a Jewish student in the Third Reich contains a German teacher as one of its characters, that figure should exhibit the traits of a typical German teacher from that period, if a movie shows the sufferings of a

Jewish family it should not end with an unu-
sually lenient fate for them. An SS officer in a
story about persecution and annihilation should
be the typical SS officer, and a movie or book
about a German helping a Jew should make
clear that such help was exceptional.

I agree that an atypical character, a non-
representative situation, or an exceptional turn
of events may be presented in a way that distorts the truth. And yet there may still be good
reasons for liking those stories. Take von Don-
nersmarck's recent film *The Lives of Others*,
which is set in the waning years of the GDR. In
it a Stasi officer assigned to spy on a playwright
comes to admire his life and to see the beauty
of art and the value of freedom. In doing so he
recognises that what he does is evil and helps
the playwright whom he is supposed to control
and denounce. The film definitely distorts the
truth; the good Stasi officer is a fairytale figure. But the film was praised and well-liked in
Germany as well as abroad; it was a fairytale
that reconciled the still-divided East and West
Germans, and it invited viewers abroad to set
the legacy of the Cold War to rest. Its healing

message that there is always some good in the bad was irresistible.

Often enough it is not the presentation of an atypical character that distorts the truth but the creation of an overly typical one. Where the typical character simply doesn't exist, creating a stereotype is a distortion of the truth. It is what propaganda movies do. In Harlan's 1940 film *Jud Süß*, a Jew who finances and ruins a German state in the eighteenth century is presented as the quintessential Jew and the Germans, decent and patient until they are finally driven to stand up and fight, as the quintessential Germans. Also I remember 1950s Westerns where Native Americans all looked the same and acted the same – colourful, noisy, easily drunk, happily cruel, and, when push came to shove, not up to the white man's bravery and decency. Those Westerns supported stereotypes that distorted the truth for a generation of viewers.

The danger of creating stereotypes can be even greater than the danger of not paying tribute to what's typical. After all, the world is more diverse than uniform. Individuals, even if they belong to the same race, the same nation, and the same religion are more diverse than uniform. Goodness is more diverse than uniform. Evil is more diverse than uniform. In his recent novel *The Kindly Ones*, which was both praised and criticised as provoking and scandalising, the French-American-Jewish author Jonathan Littell presents an SS officer's career and inner life because, as he explains in an interview that I read, he wanted to find out what evil is from the inside. But there are as many insides of evil as there are evil people and there isn't that much to find out about them. Once an SS officer or soldier has crossed the line from being a fighter to being a murderer every additional murder is just an additional number. And they crossed the line for all kinds of reasons: they got a kick out of crossing it or they thought they had to cross it, they wanted to act like their fellow soldiers, they were used to obeying orders, they didn't want or didn't dare to question them, they were convinced that it was the right thing to kill Jews, they were drunk, murdering was less dangerous than fighting, they just didn't care what they did, and so on. And the psychological predispositions that enabled them to enjoy crossing the line or to want to obey orders or not to care were as manifold as the reasons for doing so. To create the typical evil-doer is as simplistic and misleading as creating any other stereotype.

As an author I was often criticised for depicting Hanna, the woman protagonist of my novel *The Reader*, a former concentration camp guard who committed monstrous crimes, with a human face. I understand the desire for a world where those who commit monstrous crimes are always monsters. We all have the deeply-rooted expectation that a person's acts and character, outer and inner appearance, behaviour in one context and behaviour in another context should conform. Whatever sociological role theory teaches us – deep down we still have the old notion of personal identity as consistency of character, appearance and behaviour. Our language reveals this when we talk about someone looking beautiful but being awful, looking warm but being cold, looking cultured but being amoral. We don't easily talk about people looking beautiful and being awful, looking warm and being cold, looking cultured and being amoral.

But the world is full of this tension. Not seeing its multifaceted nature is simplistic and misleading. Maybe I insist on this point so strongly because my generation experienced again and again that someone whom we loved and respected turned out to have done something horrible during the Third Reich. I remember my English and gym teacher, a wonderful teacher to whom I owe my early love for the English language and also an early insight into the relativity of justice. When, at the end of the school year 1958 or 1959, my final grade in English was lower than the grades that I had gotten over the year, I asked him for an explanation. 'Schlink,' he said, 'as long as you don't try harder in sports, you won't get a better grade in English either.' I found this unfair, and of course it wasn't fair. But it showed an old pedagogue's insight into his student's psyche. I was an arrogant little intellectual and hadn't seen a reason why I should try harder in sports. Now I saw one and actually managed to swirl around the high pole that you have to jump up to. During training we students saw the tattoo on his arm that all SS officers and soldiers had that indicated the person's blood group. But it was the fifties, and we still believed that the Waffen SS was just an elite troop and that only the Concentration Camp SS was bad. Even if we had known better, we wouldn't have suspected his involvement in crimes of the Gestapo, the secret police, that only came out after his retirement.

I remember the nights that I worked in a factory as a student in the 1960s. I had a twelve-hour shift, I worked a day from six am to six pm, had twenty-four hours off, and then worked a night from six pm to six am. My impressions of my fellow workers, who had all fought in the Second World War, were always as nice, decent and helpful people. But in the hours between two am and five am they sometimes talked about the war and where, when, how and in what capacity they had been involved. They didn't talk in detail, but it was very clear that some had been involved in evil things that they could neither forget nor repress. I am sure that even in those war years, when they were at home with their families and friends, they put on the same nice faces that I saw at work.

And I remember the professor whose class I attended in my third year at law school and through whom I came to understand that studying law is more than studying articles and paragraphs; that it includes history and philosophy and is a rich intellectual universe. After my exam I started reading the legal literature from the Third Reich that, during my years of study, had been locked away in the so-called poison closet and had become available only as a concession to the rebellious students of 1968. And there they were, his writings on the totalitarian state and its necessary homogeneity and exclusion of the other, the Jew, the enemy.

No, sticking with what appears typical is no guarantee for truth: nor is avoiding it. My impression is that the demand for fiction to be representative by presenting typical characters and situations doesn't come out of a concern for the truth but rather for keeping up a precious image of events. It arises from the fear that writing about Germans as victims might damage the image of Germans as perpetrators, that writing about collaboration in the German-occupied countries might relativise German responsibility, that writing about the *Judenräte*, the Jewish councils required by the SS to govern affairs within the ghettos, might damage the image of Jewish suffering, and so forth. Again I understand the impulse. It is the same impulse that makes us tell legends, myths and fairytales. Yet I don't believe in avoiding or suppressing the tension that reality holds for us. Germans were perpetrators and also victims, the people in the occupied countries were suppressed and also collaborated, Jews suffered and were also involved. Since the tension is already there, an image free of tension couldn't be upheld in the long run even if it served a noble cause. What can and should be upheld and strived for is not a reduced but a complete image where the involvement of the *Judenräte* is not suppressed but explained, where the fact that Germans were victims is not meant to insinuate any excuse, and where collaboration is shown as a companion to each and every occupation – as is, in one form or other, resistance. The truth is not protected by presenting only what's typical. The atypical is also part of the truth – as long as it is presented and explained for what it is: atypical.

Once more: I understand the impulse to defend a precious image of events. It is similar to the impulse to tell and to preserve myths, legends, and fairytales. They can serve good purposes; *The Lives of Others* was, for my still-divided country, the right film at the right moment. Legends can inspire and encourage us, and founding myths can hold nations together. But they can do so without pretending to be the whole truth. We don't have to fear that they will lose their power in the bright light of truth.

At the beginning of this essay I mentioned not only people who want their truth about the Holocaust to be acknowledged but also those who want their trauma to be respected and to have their dignity restored. Can this give rise to the demand that fiction dealing with the Holocaust has to be not only true but also acknowledging, respectful and restorative? I don't think so. I think that truth is the only

acknowledgment, the only respect, the only restoration that fiction can provide. Yes, fiction
can have mythical, legendary and fairytale qualities that can be useful for many purposes, but
I don't think that myths, legends and fairytales
can be demanded and constructed to serve the
wants of those who have been traumatised and
persecuted during the Holocaust.

What does it mean to find truth within a
work of fiction? Fiction is true if it presents
what happened or could have happened, and
if it is a comedy or a satire, a legend, a myth
or a fairytale that opens our eyes to something
that happened or could have happened. What
it presents doesn't have to be the full truth; it
can be just a tiny element of the truth as long
as it doesn't pretend to be more than it is. And
of course, the presentation of what happened
or could have happened is far from being all
that fiction does. We don't want fiction just for
the facts being presented to us. We want reality to be presented to us and explained to us
and turned into something that, even though it
is not our reality, we can imagine ourselves into.
We read because we want to share the lives of

those we read about, we want to empathise with them, fall in love with them, train our hatred on them, and ultimately learn about ourselves from them.

Even though the composition of these fictitious realities with their fictitious plots and situations and characters is something other than a presentation of facts, I experience it as something that has to be true. I don't mean true by virtue of laying out what happened or could have happened any more – right now I mean a different truth. To be honest, I don't know exactly what I mean and how to define this truth. What I am talking about is the feeling I have when a story that I have thought about, played with, thought about some more, and played with some more is finally ready to be written. It is a feeling as strong as when, after having researched a fact extensively and carefully, I have finally found the truth. The feeling doesn't have to do with me putting something autobiographical or something else of which I am particularly certain into the story that I am going to tell. It doesn't concern having a message I want to convey that I am finally about to convey successfully or with any other agenda. It is a feeling devoid of any agenda except: now I have it, now I can tell it. And it feels like I have found the truth.

In fact, an agenda other than telling the story would, at least for me, make the feeling of truth that I try to describe impossible. Once in my life, many years ago, I had a purpose other than telling a story when I tried to write a novel. I had been left by a woman I loved. I hoped to get her back, and to have God on my side, I promised to write something in His praise if He would help me – like Franz Werfel fleeing from Vichy France to the USA promised to write and later wrote *The Song of Bernadette* about the girl that had the revelation of Maria at Lourdes. I then started to think about what to write, and came up with all kinds of ideas about stories touching on religion but none praising God and none any good. The purpose killed all creative fantasy. I don't want to go so far as to say that I was happy that the woman didn't come back to me, but there was some relief in not having a promise I had to keep.

The pursuit of truth needs no other purpose than the truth. This is evident in the well-defined truth that I first talked about: truth in fiction that represents or opens our eyes to what happened or could have happened. It also holds for the truth that I find difficult to define, for which I can give no criteria other than my feeling and the absence of an agenda. To be true in both senses is the only obligation that I can see for fiction about the Holocaust or any other traumatic past. To be precise, it is the only obligation I can see having for myself. I don't mean to say that others shouldn't write myths, legends, and fairytales about the Holocaust. But I think that not everyone is entitled to the loose play with the truth that writing myths, legends and fairytales implies. Creating myths shouldn't happen at someone else's expense; the truth that is omitted or distorted shouldn't be the truth that someone else rightly cares about. That's why I understand that *The Lives of Others* was criticised by people who felt betrayed and belittled; they had been subjected to Stasi persecution and argued convincingly that the real world under Stasi oppression would have looked different and better if characters like the good Stasi officer from *The Lives of Others* had actually existed. But I also understand the argument that can be made in the director's favour: the film's fairytale did so much good and the victims of Stasi persecution have so often been recognised that their hurt over the film can be tolerated. But this weighing and balancing of interests, concerns and hurts is a tricky topic. To tell a thrilling story can easily tempt one into tolerating someone else's hurt too easily.

As I mentioned in the introduction, the thoughts I have presented here were triggered by the questions I have been asked and the criticism I have received long after my actual writing. Even now I cannot say that those same thoughts will be with me in the future when I set out to write another book. Epistemologists distinguish between the context or logic of discovery and the context or logic of justification, and I think that most writers work in the context of discovery rather than in the context of justification. I think the delineation that I have tried to identify between more and less acceptable fictional depictions of the past within this essay is more of an unconscious presence for us than a conscious one.

I think this is true for all the delineations between morally acceptable and morally unacceptable fictional depictions of other people and their lives. I mentioned the German penal code article on Holocaust-denial, let me mention another German attempt to make what's immoral illegal. Under German law a person must not be misrepresented in a way that violates his or her integrity and dignity. In 1971 Germany's Federal Constitutional Court ruled that Klaus Mann's novel *Mephisto* must not be published, because the diabolic protagonist's ruthless career in the Third Reich was modelled after the actor Gustav Gründgens's career and therefore posthumously violated the personality of Gründgens, who had died eight years ago. In 2007 the court ruled that Maxim Biller's novel *Esra* must not be published, because here the female protagonist and her mother were modelled after the author's former girlfriend and her mother, modelled with such malice and hatred that again the daughter's and the mother's personalities were violated. Both decisions received much public attention and legal discussion; I myself have doubts whether the law should get involved in the arts like that. But I haven't found anyone who didn't agree on the moral aspect. Klaus Mann hadn't overstepped the line between what's morally acceptable and what's unacceptable; his sister had been involved with and traumatised by Gründgens, he and his sister had to leave Germany while Gründgens made a ruthless career, and he was strong enough to take care of his interests. Maxim Biller's protagonist couldn't fight back, she hadn't done anything bad that justified her malicious depiction. And while the normal reader would hardly remember Gründgens, who had died in 1963, while reading *Mephisto* in and after 1971, Biller himself had created a media hype that made everybody know that *Esra* was a book about his former girlfriend. He defended what he had written as a writer's artistic privilege, but in such a shrill tone that I found it obvious that he knew that he had crossed the line. The moral issue was clear without much weighing and balancing of interests, concerns and hurts. In writing, as in other areas of life, what is moral is mostly self-evident.

Acknowledgments

The essays in this book were the six Lord Weiden-feld Lectures given at St Anne's College, Oxford in 2008. I thank the community of fellows and students at St Anne's and its principal, Tim Gardam, for an inspiring and rewarding stay.

Thanks go to Joyce Hackett and Julia Steinmetz. Julia Steinmetz, fellow lawyer and fellow writer, translated my German publications which I used to draft my essays with competence and sensitivity. Joyce Hackett, novelist, essayist and great friend, helped clarify my thoughts, sharpen my words and give the essays their final shape.

About the Author

BERNHARD SCHLINK has published several works of fiction and nonfiction. His novel *The Reader* was an international bestseller, won multiple prestigious literary prizes, has been translated into more than thirty-seven languages, and was made into an Academy Award–winning film. His most recent novel, *Homecoming*, was published in 2008 to critical acclaim. Bernhard Schlink divides his time between New York and Berlin.